Leo Tolstoy

Titles in the series Critical Lives present the work of leading cultural figures of the modern period. Each book explores the life of the artist, writer, philosopher or architect in question and relates it to their major works.

In the same series

Leo Tolstoy

Andrei Zorin

REAKTION BOOKS

In memory of Boris (Barukh) Berman

Published by Reaktion Books Ltd
Unit 32, Waterside
44–48 Wharf Road
London N1 7UX, UK

www.reaktionbooks.co.uk

First published 2020
Copyright © Andrei Zorin 2020

Printed and bound in India by Replika Press Pvt. Ltd

A catalogue record for this book is available from the British Library

ISBN 978 1 78914 199 3

Contents

Abbreviations

AK	Leo Tolstoy, *Anna Karenina*, trans. George Gibian (London and New York, 1995)
AT	Alexandra Tolstoy, *Otets. Zhizn' L'va Tolstogo*, 2 vols (New York, 1953)
Ch-Ls	Anton Chekhov, *A. P. Polnoe sobranie sochinenii i pisem: Pis'ma v dvenadtsati tomah*, 12 vols (Moscow, 1974–83)
CW	Leo Tolstoy, *Polnoe sobranie sochinenii*, 90 vols (Moscow, 1928–64)
Ds	*Tolstoy's Diaries*, trans. R. F. Christian (London, 1994)
Kuz	Tatiana Kuzminskaya, *Moia zhizn' doma i v Yasnoi Polyane* (Tula, 1973)
LNT & AAT	*L. N. Tolstoy i A. A. Tolstaya: Perepiska, 1857–1903* (Moscow, 2011)
Ls	*Tolstoy's Letters*, ed. and trans. R. F. Christian, 2 vols (New York, 1978)
Mak	Dushan Makovitsky, 'U Tolstogo, 1904–1910: Yasnopolianskie zapiski', *Literaturnoe nasledstvo*, xc/1–4 (1979)
SAT-DS	Sofia Tolstaya, *Dnevniki*, 2 vols (Moscow, 1978)
SAT-ML	Sofia Tolstaya, *Moia zhizn'*, 2 vols (Moscow, 2011)
TP	Leo Tolstoy, *Perepiska s russkimi pisateliami*, ed. S. Rozanova, 2 vols (Moscow, 1978)
TSF	*Tolstoy's Short Fiction*, trans. Michael Kats (London and New York, 2008)
WP	Leo Tolstoy, *War and Peace*, trans. George Gibian (London and New York, 1996).

1

An Ambitious Orphan

In May 1878, finishing *Anna Karenina* and in the early stages of the deepest spiritual crisis he had ever experienced, Tolstoy started drafting his memoirs, which he provisionally called *My Life*. In one day he wrote several disjointed fragments describing his impressions of certain events from his childhood. He did not complete his memoirs and never returned to these fragments, the first of which was as follows:

> Here are my first recollections. I am bound up, I want to free my hands and I cannot do it. I shout and weep and my cries are unpleasant to me, but I cannot stop. There were people bent over me, I do not remember who they were, and it all happened in semi-darkness, but I do remember that there were two of them, they are worried by my cries, but do not unbind me, which I want them to do, and therefore I cry even louder. It seems that for them it is necessary [that I must be bound up], while I know that it is not necessary, and I want to prove it to them and I indulge in crying that repels me, but which is uncontainable. I feel the injustice and cruelty not of people, because they pity me, but of fate and pity for myself. I do not know and shall never know what this was about . . . but it is certain that this was the first and the most powerful impression of my life. And what is memorable is not my cries, or my suffering, but the complex, contradictory nature of the impression. I want

freedom, it won't harm anyone and yet they keep torturing me. They pity me and they tie me up, and I, who needs everything, am weak and they are strong. (*cw*, XXIII, pp. 469–70)

This episode does not provide material for psychoanalytic speculation. Tolstoy's 'first and most powerful impression' was not extracted from the depths of his subconscious on an analyst's couch. It is a conscious (re)construction carried out by a fifty-year-old writer. Tolstoy describes himself as a baby, but 'remembers' the subtlety and complexity of his lived experience, and the most powerful part of this experience is the feeling of being bound up and unfree. Tolstoy pays special attention to the love and pity shown by the adults towards him, describing their attitude as a kind of cruelty born of care. The infant Tolstoy strives to free himself from this well-intentioned despotism, but is too weak to overcome the power of those who show their concern by not allowing him to move. This struggle was to permeate the author's entire life right up until his final moments.

A conventional biography usually starts with the family origins of its subject. In the case of Leo (Lev Nikolaevich) Tolstoy, this is both essential and redundant. It is redundant because one of Tolstoy's greatest novels, *War and Peace*, provides such a powerful and memorable description of the writer's ancestors that any reality is bound to pale in comparison. It is essential because Tolstoy's family history informs the novel and in many ways defines his biography. In what is a hallmark of his writing, Tolstoy blurs the line between fiction and 'real life' by marginally changing the names of the characters. Thus the Volkonskys, the real family name of Tolstoy's mother, transform into the Bolkonskys. The Volkonskys were one of the most aristocratic families of the land, stemming from the ninth-century Varangian prince Rurik, semi-legendary founder of Russian statehood. The wordplay on Tolstoy's paternal family name

Tolstoy in 1878–9.

is a bit more complex. In an early draft of *War and Peace* it appears as Tolstov and in later drafts changed into Prostov ('The Simple one' in Russian), but this name smacked too much of an eighteenth-century moralistic comedy. By omitting the first letter, Tolstoy arrived at Rostov, a surname sounding like the ancient Russian town, thus underlining the national roots of the family. This change notwithstanding, simplicity remains a fundamental feature of the Rostovs' way of life in the novel.

To a modern reader, the title of count sits oddly with simple habits and democratic origin. However, this title had been awarded to Russian nobles only since the beginning of the eighteenth century and thus pointed to a relatively short family history. In fact, the marriage between Tolstoy's parents – and the novel's principal characters – was a misalliance: Princess Maria Volkonsky was a rich heiress; her husband, Count Nikolai Tolstoy, was on the brink of ruin, thanks to his father's profligate lifestyle. She married at the age of 32, in 1822, a year after the death of her father. By the standards of her time she was already a spinster and, according to Tolstoy, 'not good looking'. Her husband was four years her junior. In the novel Tolstoy does not conceal the practical reasons behind the marriage but these do not obscure the mutual love in a marriage made in Heaven. We don't know whether the family life of Tolstoy's parents resembled the blissful union portrayed in the Epilogue to *War and Peace*. Even if Tolstoy's father's reputation as a womanizer is unfair, we know that he spent most of the time away from home settling endless legal disputes in court or hunting in nearby forests. His wife, meanwhile, had built a special gazebo in the park where she would wait for her missing husband.

For Tolstoy, writing in his unfinished memoirs, his mother was a perfect wife who did not actually love her husband. Her heart fully belonged to her children, especially the eldest, Nikolai, and Leo, her fourth and youngest son. Born on 28 August 1828, Leo was barely two years old when his mother died a few months after the birth of her only daughter Maria.

This early loss had a profound impact on Tolstoy. He worshipped the memory of his mother and made a point of spending time in her favourite corner of the family garden. He would later insist that his wife deliver their children on the same sofa on which he was born and, most importantly, forever longed for the maternal love of which he had been deprived. Tolstoy could not remember his mother and was glad that no portraits of her were preserved by the family, except for a miniature silhouette cut from black paper. His ideal spiritual image of the person he loved most would thus remain untainted by material artefacts. Fighting temptations 'in the middle period of his life', Tolstoy recalled that he prayed to the soul of his mother and the prayers always helped.

In 1906, aged 77, Tolstoy wrote in his diary:

Was in the dull miserable state all day. By evening, this state changed to one of emotion – the desire for affection – for love. I felt as in childhood like clinging to a loving pitying creature, and weeping emotionally and being comforted. But who is the creature I could cling to like that. I ran through all the people I love – nobody would do. Who could I cling to? I wanted to be young again and cling to my mother as I imagine her to have been. Yes, yes, my dear mother whom I never called by this name since I could not talk. Yes, she is my highest conception of pure love – not the cold and divine, but a warm, earthly, maternal love. This is what attracts my better, weary soul. Mother dear, caress me. All this is stupid, but it is true. (*Ds*, pp. 395–6)

An acute awareness of his status as an orphan haunted Tolstoy throughout his life. This was aggravated by the early death of his father in June 1837 when Leo was approaching his ninth birthday.

Silhouette of Tolstoy's mother, 1800s.

The count died suddenly of a stroke during a trip to Tula. There was a suspicion that he had been poisoned by servants. Later Tolstoy said that he never believed these rumours, but was aware of them and must have been deeply affected by the talk of such a crime. These losses most likely contributed to the extreme shyness and sensitivity of Tolstoy, who was known to his relatives as a crybaby. Young Leo was also lagging behind his brothers in studies and was deeply traumatized by his physical unattractiveness. This self-deprecation persisted through his youth: at least until his marriage Tolstoy did not believe that any woman could ever fall in love with such an ugly person as himself – so much for the image of Tolstoy's blissful happiness as a boy. Yet, while the image may have not been grounded in reality, it was grounded in his literary imagination.

The idyllic picture of his early years is most vividly recreated in *Childhood*, the 1852 novel that brought Tolstoy national literary fame. This exquisite and touching description of the life of an aristocratic boy abounds with autobiographical details and until the present day informs our perception of Tolstoy's environment, thoughts and feelings in Yasnaya Polyana ('The Clear Glade'), the family estate near the city of Tula where he spent his formative years. The idyll he describes in *Childhood* ends with the sudden death of the narrator's mother. *Adolescence* and *Youth*, the next parts of Tolstoy's autobiographical trilogy, tell a very different story of psychological difficulties, doubts and hardships.

In *Childhood* Tolstoy transforms the first and most tragic loss of his life from the early, crushing yet unremembered trauma of a two-year-old into the formative experience of an eleven-year-old boy. This chronological move enables him to portray the joys of childhood that precede the death of the boy's mother as pure and unmixed with the feelings of deprivation and loneliness that the real Leo experienced from the dawn of his remembered days. The idyllic world of *Childhood* is as much of a myth as the ideal family described in the Epilogue to *War and Peace*.

Yasnaya Polyana also remained for Tolstoy mysteriously connected with the vision of universal happiness. Speaking about Tolstoy's childhood, no biographer ever fails to mention the story of the green stick. During their games, Leo's elder brother Nikolai would tell his younger siblings that a magic green stick hidden somewhere nearby would make the person lucky enough to find it able to make all humans happy. Little Leo was deeply impressed. He never abandoned his belief in the green stick and the search for it. Several years before his death, he wrote in his memoirs:

> as I knew then, that there is the green stick with the
> inscription that tells us how to destroy all evil in humans
> and give them the greatest good, I believe now that
> this is the truth and it will be opened to humans and
> give them all that it promises. (*cw*, xxxiv, p. 386)

Around the same time he chose to call an article on his religious opinions 'The Green Stick'. In his will, Tolstoy also asked to be buried near the place where as a boy he had searched for this treasure.

Numerous female relatives took care of the orphaned siblings. One of them, Tatiana Ergolskaya, usually called Toinette, became for Leo the spirit of Yasnaya Polyana. Brought up as a poor relative in the family of Tolstoy's grandparents, Toinette was in love with Tolstoy's father, her second cousin. In an act of self-sacrifice, she had renounced her feelings to allow her beloved Nikolai to marry an heiress. In 1836, a year before his death, hoping to give his children a stepmother who would never leave them, the widowed count proposed to Ergolskaya. She declined, but nonetheless eagerly shouldered the burden of caring for the Tolstoy children. Leo was her clear favourite. Her dubious status in the family is reflected in an unflattering portrait of Sonya's role in the Rostov household after Nikolai's marriage in *War and Peace*. Ergolskaya lived long enough to read the novel, but her reaction to it remains unknown.

Having declined the opportunity to become the children's stepmother, Ergolskaya also lost the right to be their legal guardian. The sisters of Tolstoy's father were both considered closer to their nephews. When one aunt, Alexandra Osten-Saken, died in 1841 the children were entrusted to another, Pelageya (Polina) Yushkova, who lived in Kazan. This town on the Volga river, home to one of the six universities in the Russian Empire, seemed a suitable place for the growing children. Kazan was a natural centre for Oriental studies, given that the town and its surrounding region was home to the Volga Tatars, the empire's largest Muslim minority. After failing to gain admission on his first attempt, Leo was admitted to the Faculty of Oriental Languages when he applied again in 1844.

The main challenges of Tolstoy's teenage life coincided with the five and a half years he lived in Kazan. First and foremost, he had to handle the conflict between his powerful sexuality and a no less powerful desire for chastity. He knew very well that it was Eros that had ruined the primordial innocence of humanity. In *Childhood*, Tolstoy describes with the lofty tenderness of an experienced man the emerging erotic feelings of a ten-year-old boy suddenly kissing a girl's naked shoulder. Expelled from the paradise of early childhood, he must now deal with less touching and delicate emotions.

In Kazan Tolstoy was relatively free from the control of his relatives. Although not rich, he still had money to spend. At the same time, he was extremely shy and unsure of himself, especially in the company of women of his own social standing. Inevitably this combination of factors made him a regular visitor to brothels. Introduced to paid sex by his elder brother at the age of fifteen, Leo would later recall standing weeping by the bed after losing his virginity. This tension between irresistible lust and revulsion, chiefly for his own bestiality, became a recurrent emotional theme, first in his diaries and then in his prose.

Tellingly, it was while being treated for gonorrhoea at the university clinic in 1847 that Tolstoy began the diary he would continue to keep, on and off, for the next sixty years. The most significant interruption coincided with the period he was working on his two main novels. The diary exposes to harsh scrutiny not only the author's deeds, but his secret thoughts and desires. The level of maniacal self-absorption and self-flagellation to which Tolstoy subjects himself can be shocking to a modern reader. Seeking to live by the highest moral criteria, he sets himself impossible tasks and, time and again, chastises himself for failing to meet them. Reading the diary, one is reminded of Philippe Lejeune's observation that 'a diary is rarely a self-portrait, or if it is taken as one, it sometimes seems like a caricature.'[1]

Tolstoy's diary does not represent the person we come to know from many of his letters and the memoirs of his friends and family members: charmingly or caustically witty, tenderly, if sometimes awkwardly, caring about the people he loved, actively generous and kind. The most difficult and sometimes unappealing traits of Tolstoy's personality most strongly reveal themselves in the intimate spheres of his life: the diary and in his relations with his wife. Often these two spheres overlap.

In his first diary entry we can already observe the outline of Tolstoy's future struggles with his own persona:

> I've come to see clearly that the disorderly life that the majority of fashionable people take to be a consequence of youth is nothing other than a consequence of the early corruption of the soul . . . Let a man withdraw from society, let him retreat into himself, and his reason will soon cast aside the spectacles which showed him everything in distorted form and his view of things will become so clear that he will be unable to understand how he had not seen it before. Let reason do its work and it will indicate to you your destiny, and will give you rules with which you can confidently enter society . . . Form your reason so that it would be coherent with the whole, the source of everything, and not with the part, i.e. the society of people, then the society as a part won't have an influence on you. It is easier to write ten volumes of philosophy than to put one single principle into practice. (*Ds*, p. 4; *cw*, xlvi, p. 3)

These early and somewhat amusing deliberations already show Tolstoy in miniature – from any occasion, however trivial it may seem, he is ready to derive major conclusions about humankind. He is certain that proper introspection can serve as a clue to the whole of humanity as any individual person is a part of the whole, and that reason alone is sufficient to perform this work. He believes that the truth is self-evident for a person who is independent from the corrupting influence of society. At the same time, he wants both to enter society and to mend it according to his ideas. He is also confident that philosophy is useful only if it serves practical needs and shapes the moral life of a person.

Further entries are written along the same lines. In one of them, the nineteen-year-old Tolstoy sets himself the task of mastering most of the existing sciences and arts, namely law, medicine, agriculture (both theoretical and practical), history, geography, statistics, mathematics, natural sciences, music and painting. In addition to that, he wants to study six languages and to write a dissertation and essays 'on all the subjects he was going to study'. To give these ambitions an air of relative realism, Tolstoy explains that he wants to explore these fields with different degrees of depth: in music and painting, for example, he aspires to attain only 'an average degree of perfection'. One of the most important tasks Tolstoy sets himself is 'to write down rules'. Within several months he drafted rules for developing the physical will, emotional will, rational will, memory, activity and intellectual faculties. The first rule he prescribed to himself was 'independence from all extraneous circumstances' and avoidance of 'the society of women' (*Ds*, pp. 6–7). Predictably, he did not succeed in either.

In his studies Tolstoy always excelled at languages; a quarter of a century later the speed with which he learned ancient Greek seemed unbelievable to classical scholars. He did well in Tatar-Turkish (as the language was listed in the curriculum) and in Arabic, both of which he soon forgot, but failed other subjects including Russian history. Reluctant to resit the exams, Tolstoy applied for a transfer to the law faculty, but did not succeed there either. In 1847, when he came of age and entered his inheritance, he resigned from the university without receiving a degree. Fortunately the partition of the family property among his siblings left him with Yasnaya Polyana. Immediately he rushed back to join his aunt Toinette.

All these sporadic impulses, hopes and disappointments clearly reveal the influence of Rousseau. Tolstoy, as he later confessed, worshipped the Genevan thinker and even dreamt of wearing a medallion with Rousseau's face. He shared Rousseau's passionate cult of nature and a belief that the original purity of the human being had been spoilt by the artificial demands of society and civilization. Even more important for Tolstoy was Rousseau's ideal of absolute transparency of the soul and the ensuing practice of incessant self-scrutiny, as well as his restlessness and constant readiness to run away from everything he owned or had achieved. Unlike Rousseau, however, Tolstoy was never a homeless wanderer. Yasnaya Polyana, through the vastness and beauty of its landscapes, through familial lore and strong ties with people of the land, connected him with the history and essence of Russia. Prodigal sons are doomed to leave their paradise behind, but Tolstoy, though he left it many times, always returned to Yasnaya Polyana. After his very last escape and subsequent death, his body was brought back to be buried in his native soil.

For several years Tolstoy oscillated between Yasnaya Polyana, Tula (where, surprisingly for such a born anarchist, he procured a sinecure in the civil service), Moscow and St Petersburg. In the capitals he aspired to learn manners and behaviour that would make him respectable in high society, but as was often the case with Tolstoy, his diary records both a fascination for the aristocratic world and a countervailing revulsion. Much later, describing the corrupt received opinions of his social milieu, Tolstoy wrote that

Tolstoy as a teenager, 1840s – the earliest-known drawing of Tolstoy.

Entrance to Yasnaya Polyana, 1892.

'the kind aunt with whom I lived [Ergolskaya], herself the purest of beings, always told me that there was nothing she so desired for me as that I should have relations with a married woman: "Rien ne forme un jeune homme, comme une liaison avec une femme comme il faut"' (CW, XXIII, p. 4).

Tolstoy confessed that in 'yielding to the passions' he felt that the society approved of him. However, most of the dubious habits he acquired, like drinking, feasting and gambling, were more the marks of a hussar than of polished patrician venality. 'Improving' liaisons with high-status women evaded Leo. For more than a decade he sought sexual gratification mostly with prostitutes, servants, peasants, Gypsy and Cossack girls. In *Youth*, the last part of his autobiographical trilogy, we see that 'les hommes comme il faut' interested him more than 'les femmes comme il faut'.

'I have never been in love with women,' he wrote in his diary in November 1851:

I have been very often in love with men . . . I fell in love with men before I had any idea of the possibility of pederasty; but even when I knew about it, the possibility of coitus never occurred to me . . . My love for Islavin spoilt the whole of eight months of my life in Petersburg for me . . . I always loved the sort of people who were cool towards me and only took me for what I was worth . . . Beauty always had a lot of influence on my choice; however, there is the case with Dyakov; but I'll never forget the night we were travelling from Pirogovo, and wrapped up underneath a travelling rug, I wanted to kiss him and cry. There was sensuality in that feeling, but why it took this course it is impossible to decide, because, as I said, my imagination never painted a lubricious picture; on the contrary I have a terrible aversion to all that. (*Ds*, p. 32)

As in most cases, one can get more insight into Tolstoy's personality by listening to what he actually says than by attempting to

The general view of Yasnaya Polyana, 1897.

psychoanalyse him. An ideal male, so different socially from the women that aroused his desire, represents a vision of the person the diarist himself painfully and hopelessly aspired to become. Both Tolstoy's great novels have the same pairing of lead male characters projecting two halves of the authorial alter ego: the good-hearted, passionate but awkward and slightly boorish Pierre and Levin are juxtaposed with the brilliant and polished noblemen Prince Andrei and Vronsky. The latter, typically of their peers, were army officers. Tolstoy's brother and mentor Nikolai was also doing military service. It was all but inevitable that, at some point, Leo would try to take the same path.

Tolstoy's life in the army falls into two distinct phases: the Caucasus and the Crimea. In April 1851, having lost more at the gambling table than he could afford to repay, Tolstoy followed Nikolai to the Caucasus. For more than two years he was based in the Cossack settlement at Starogladkovskaya, initially as a sort of intern attached to the regiment and then as an artillery officer. During these years he took part in many raids against the Chechens and deeply immersed himself in the exotic Cossack way of life. By the time Tolstoy arrived at the frontier, the war in the Caucasus between the Russian Empire and parts of the indigenous population had been going on for more than thirty years. At the beginning of the nineteenth century Russia had finally managed to prevail over the Ottoman and Persian empires and establish control of the mostly Christian principalities south of the Caucasus Mountains. However, communications with the newly acquired territories were constantly disrupted by rebellious, mostly Islamic, tribes from the mountains.

Russian troops were quartered in the region to keep the local population under control, but the long, porous border forced the authorities to rely upon the military assistance of the Cossacks, the settlers who for generations had combined military service with farming and agricultural activity on communally owned land. For centuries criminals, runaway serfs and those from the margins of society found refuge in the Cossacks' settlements on the borders of the empire. Fiercely independent, Cossacks were also significantly richer than the peasants in mainland Russia. Many of them, including the inhabitants of Starogladkovskaya, adhered to the Old Belief, an Orthodox confession that had been much persecuted by the official Church since the mid-seventeenth century. Cossack men lived to fight and hunt, leaving many traditionally male preoccupations, including ploughing, planting, herding and reaping, to their women, who were physically strong, morally independent and enjoyed sexual freedom unheard of among Russian lower classes of the time. Many Russian Romantic writers of the early nineteenth century wrote admiringly about the primitive, natural and warrior lifestyle shared by the Cossacks and Caucasian mountain people. Tolstoy, with his escapist temperament and penchant for all that was natural and rebellious, was fascinated by the world he discovered, describing it often in his works. With his new life came an experience that was arguably to affect his writing even more: regular proximity to death.

Death for Tolstoy was an obsession no less powerful than sex. Having first met death so early in his life, Leo could never avoid thinking about it, waiting for it, fearing and desiring it at the same time. For the soldiers, tribesmen and Cossacks he encountered in the Caucasus, death was a routine experience. Now Tolstoy had plenty of opportunity to watch people dying and, perhaps more importantly, to observe how they lived so close to death: braving it, ignoring it as an everyday preoccupation, coping with the loss of those who had spoken to them only a day, an hour, a few minutes before.

Nearly a decade after his experience in the Caucasus, Tolstoy wrote 'Three Deaths', a story that compares the death of a noble lady full of resentment, envy and condemnation for those remaining alive, with the death of a peasant fully reconciled with his own mortality, and that of a tree that readily frees its place for new vegetation. The ability of living creatures to accept death is, Tolstoy suggests, inversely related to how strongly they perceive their own uniqueness in the world. Tolstoy passionately wished to develop a peasant-like, if not tree-like, attitude to death and dissolve himself into a universal life that does not differentiate between individual beings, but his habit of painful soul-searching, need for self-assertion and quest for personal greatness were equally strong.

On 29 March 1852, while at Starogladkovskaya, he wrote in his diary:

> I am tormented by the pettiness of my life. – I feel that it
> is because I am petty myself – but I still have the strength
> to despise myself, and my life. There is something in me
> that makes me believe that I wasn't born to be the same
> as other people . . . I am still tormented by thirst . . . not
> for fame – I don't want fame and I despise it – but to have
> a big influence on people's happiness and usefulness.
> Shall I simply die with this hopeless wish? (*Ds*, p. 40)

From the beginning Tolstoy's self-reproach was inseparable from his burning ambition. In the Caucasus he regularly exposed this connection in his diary as he began to suspect that he had stumbled upon the green stick of fable. From late August 1851, before he even left for the Caucasus, Tolstoy had secretly begun to work on his first story. A failed student, dissipated landowner and low-ranking officer was discovering himself as a writer.

It was less exceptional in nineteenth-century Russia for a professional writer to emerge from the ranks of the nobility than in the rest of Western Europe. The Westernizing reforms of Peter the Great at the beginning of the eighteenth century had forced the nobility to not only change their facial hair, clothes and manners, but to acquire better education suitable for their new European lifestyles. A new educated elite that constituted the Russian nobility embraced and internalized the Petrine reforms, striving to put itself on an equal footing with its European peers. Europeanized Russian nobles not only produced the formidable officer corps that triumphed over Napoleon, but created the unique culture of Russia's Golden Age.

Still, these remarkable achievements stood on the foundation of serfdom. Only nobles could own land. They enjoyed nearly unlimited power over the peasants living on their estates. This extended to more than just the fruits of their labour. Serfs could be bought, sold, sent to military service or penal institutions, punished physically or financially and their families could be broken up at their owner's whim. Under Peter the Great and his immediate successors, when state service was mandatory for the nobles, everyone was subject to at least some form of servitude. This changed in 1762 when the nobility was allowed to choose whether to serve or not. This new freedom unleashed the cultural creativity of the most educated scions of the Russian nobility just as the Enlightenment took flight. The new ideas from Europe were starkly opposed to the moral affront of serfdom. As Russia entered the Golden Age, this contrast began to gnaw at the consciences of the nobility's brightest minds.

Young officers returning from the Napoleonic wars saw themselves as the liberators of Europe. Now more acutely aware of the lack of freedom at home, they started forming conspiratorial groups to liberate Russia. At first they aspired to help Emperor Alexander I overcome the resistance of the conservatives to the belated reforms. Later a core of conspirators started planning a full-scale military *coup d'état*. In December 1825, after the emperor's death, rebellious officers brought their regiments to the Palace Square in St Petersburg and refused to take an oath of allegiance to the new monarch. After a day of turmoil, the insurrection was dispersed with cannon. Six months later, with no formal trial, five plot leaders were sent to the gallows and dozens more to hard labour and exile in Siberia.

The Decembrists, as the conspirators came to be known, constituted a tiny minority of the nobility but the most aristocratic families were particularly prominent in their ranks. This self-sacrifice by the most privileged members of an emerging society seized the country's imagination. In the absence of any political representation or moral guidance from a Church that had long been subservient to the state, literature became the single most important channel for shaping and expressing public opinion. In 1820s and '30s Russia the dawn of the Romantic age with its search for a national spirit strongly reinforced the perception of the writer as a voice speaking on behalf of the nation before the authorities.

The early 1850s was both a difficult and exciting time to start a literary career. Emperor Nicholas I, eager to suppress any hint of dissent after the European revolutions of 1848, had begun a new round of political repression. Among many others, the young Fedor Dostoevsky was arrested, sentenced to death, pardoned on the brink of execution and sent to Siberia. Censorship became exceptionally severe. 'Why bother', said one censor surprised at the temerity of authors who persisted in writing, 'when we have already decided not to allow anything?'[2] The reading public, however, shared a feeling that the end of an epoch was approaching and major changes were in the air. New works were eagerly awaited from a cohort of young writers, including the novelists Ivan Turgenev and Ivan Goncharov, the great satirist Mikhail Saltykov-Shchedrin and the dramatist Alexander Ostrovsky, whose plays would come to form the backbone of Russian national theatre.

New writers discussed actual social problems, defying outdated Romantic conventions. They gathered around *Sovremennik* (The Contemporary), a literary magazine started in the 1830s by the poet Alexander Pushkin and later edited by Nikolai Nekrasov, one of the most universally popular poets of his age, who wrote mostly about the hard lives of Russian peasants. The publication in *Sovremennik* of Tolstoy's first novel, *Childhood*, coincided with the death of Nikolai Gogol, the leading writer of the previous generation, and the arrest of Ivan Turgenev, the most prominent voice of a new generation, for his obituary of Gogol. One can hardly imagine a more powerful symbol both of continuity and change.

Tolstoy's choice of subject-matter for his literary debut was a brilliant move, both artistically and tactically. The vision of childhood as a lost paradise was one of the most powerful myths of Romantic culture, overwhelmed by nostalgia for a golden age of innocence and unity with nature. In the social landscape of eighteenth- and nineteenth-century Europe, one could not imagine a better setting for this world of bliss than a nobleman's country estate. Rousseau had located the utopian world of Clarence in such an estate. Karl Moor, the charismatic hero of Schiller's *The Robbers*, is heir to a family castle to which he longs in vain to return. Yet if Schiller, the son of a doctor, can be said to have launched this trope into Romantic literature, it was Tolstoy, as one to the manor born, who would flesh it out with details from a world he knew so intimately well.

Russia was preparing to part with its Golden Age and was feeling nostalgic in advance. Childhood memories could serve as a safe haven under any censorship regime. At the same time they did not provoke animosity among a liberal or even a radical audience because Tolstoy found an innovative approach to this highly traditional topic. At first he intended to write his book as a conventional memoir, but a grown-up memoirist in the middle of the nineteenth century could not have failed to see the inhuman social fabric that lay beneath the idyll he was describing. Very soon Tolstoy shifted to the reconstruction of the thoughts, feelings and perceptions of a ten-year-old boy, one of the first such endeavours in world literature. Placing his book on the thin borderline between the autobiographical and fictional, he managed to present his personal experience as universal without losing a feeling of total authenticity. Later this technique would become the unmistakable trademark of Tolstoy's narratives.

Doubts about his potential as a writer tortured Tolstoy throughout work on his first masterpiece. 'I am doing nothing and thinking about the landlady,' he complained on 30 May 1852. 'Have I the talent to compare with modern Russian writers? Decidedly not.' Two days later his opinion somewhat shifted:

> Although there will be spelling mistakes in *Childhood* it will still be tolerable. My only thought about it is there are worse stories. I'm still not convinced, however, that I lack talent. I think I lack patience, experience and clarity, and there is nothing great about my feelings or my thoughts – I still have doubts, however, about the latter. (*Ds*, pp. 44–5)

Tolstoy sent the completed novel to Nekrasov accompanied by a letter marked by his characteristic mixture of extreme shyness and thinly veiled arrogance. He included in the envelope money to pay for return delivery in case of rejection and, in case of acceptance, asked for his initials to be used instead of his full name. He agreed in advance to any cuts Nekrasov would like to make, but insisted that his novel should be published 'without additions and changes' (*TP*, 1, p. 50). Nekrasov's reaction was more than obliging. He immediately published *Childhood* in the next issue of *Sovremennik*, expressed his interest in the following parts of the book and praised it highly in a letter to Turgenev, who also quickly came to admire the young writer's talent.

The critics were equally enthusiastic. Reading the reviews in a peasant hut, Tolstoy, as he later told his wife, was 'strangled by tears of rapture'.[3] In his diaries, apart from reproaching himself for idleness, gambling and sensuality, 'that did not give him a moment's peace', Tolstoy recorded his new belief in a 'brilliant literary career that is open' to him if he can 'work hard' (*Ds*, p. 56) and abstain from sex. He was to prove right on one score, even if sexual abstinence remained beyond his power. Tolstoy's work on *Boyhood*, a continuation of *Childhood*, was very intensive, but this did not prevent him from feeling a 'hopeless aversion' both to his story and to himself. *Boyhood*, published in *Sovremennik* in October 1854, was received with nearly the same kind of acclaim as *Childhood*. The public was eagerly awaiting new work from this already famous author. Tolstoy would not fail to satisfy their expectations. The new work that was to take his fame to a new level would emerge at a different period in his life when he had lived through sea changes in Russian history that would enrich his experience.

In 1853 the ailing emperor, Nicholas I, declared war on Turkey believing that he could realize a long-cherished imperial dream of establishing Russian control over the parts of the Ottoman Empire located in Europe, their Orthodox populations and the straits leading to the Mediterranean. The emperor failed to make allowance for the strength of European opposition to Russian expansion. This allowed Britain and France to forgo their ancient rivalry and back the Turks in a united military coalition. An Anglo-French army invaded the Crimea and besieged Sebastopol, Russia's main naval port on the Black Sea.

Decaying autocrats hoping to bury their failures beneath a wave of popular enthusiasm will often go to war. The strategy invariably works well at the early stages of the adventure. Russia in the 1850s was no exception. Tolstoy himself was not immune to outbursts of patriotic feeling. When the start of the Crimean War found him in the Caucasus far from the main battlefields, he applied to be transferred and was sent to the Russian army fighting in Romania. Having found out that nothing of real importance was happening there as well, he applied again for a transfer and, in November 1854, joined Russian troops in the Crimea. His first impressions were favourable. He admired the heroic spirit of the common soldiers and junior officers and was certain the enemy would not be able to capture the city. Within two weeks, however, he had changed his mind and became 'more convinced than before that Russia must either fall or be completely transformed' (*Ds*, p. 83). He considered proposing far-reaching military reforms, but then reverted to the activity he knew best.

Tolstoy's new military experience was different. In the Caucasus, where the Russian army had an overwhelming edge over the tribesmen, both in numbers and weapons, he had participated only in sporadic raids. Mortal danger was always present and real, but could be reduced, if not avoided, by reasonable caution. The actual casualty rate was relatively low. In Sebastopol Russian officers, soldiers and even the ordinary inhabitants of the city had to withstand regular artillery fire from an enemy using the most sophisticated military technology. Death and mutilation were a daily routine and a matter of pure chance. Those who survived on a given day were just more fortunate than those who were killed or maimed. They remained subject to the same kind of dreadful lottery the next day.

By March 1855, two months after the demise of Nicholas I, apparently broken by military setbacks, Tolstoy finished the first of his Sebastopol stories. It was published in *Sovremennik* in June under the title 'Sebastopol in December'. Afraid of losing face, the new emperor Alexander II prolonged the war before finally capitulating in 1856. By this time Tolstoy had published two more stories in *Sovremennik*: 'Sebastopol in May' and 'Sebastopol in August'.

In his stories Tolstoy portrays a city getting on with its regular life at a time of death and destruction. Peasant women sell buns in the crowd on the embankment within immediate reach of the French artillery. A girl jumps across the street trying not to get her pink dress wet near a noble club that had been turned into

Siege of Sebastopol, drawing by Vasily Timm, 1854–5.

a hospital for the wounded. Officers are chasing pretty girls and telling dirty stories, knowing that in an hour they will go to the bastion, possibly never to return. Moreover, Tolstoy showed that the sense of duty and self-sacrifice involved in being ready to die for one's country are compatible with, indeed are actually inseparable from, self-assertion, petty vanity, desire for promotion or the wish to show off to one's peers.

Developing the technique he had discovered in *Childhood*, Tolstoy brought together fictional heroes and a more than real narrator who shares with the reader his personal experience and offers a sort of on-site journalistic reportage accompanied by moralistic comments, psychological observations and philosophical conclusions. This combination allowed him to present almost as documentary evidence the inner motives and impulses of his characters, including the last thoughts and feelings of the dying. The reader familiar with *War and Peace* or any literary description of twentieth-century wars will struggle to see the striking novelty of Tolstoy's approach, but the mid-nineteenth-century reading public in Russia or anywhere else had never encountered anything remotely similar. In *Childhood* Tolstoy found the new techniques to speak about a vanishing civilization. In the Sebastopol stories he discovered ways to describe new warfare with its indiscriminate destruction, blurring of the lines between the battlefield and ordinary life, and indifference to the passing of any single individual, whom he portrays as a mere drop in an ocean of death.

Tolstoy's narrative strategy remained the same throughout the whole cycle, but the actual content of each story depended upon the stages of war. 'Sebastopol in December' was devoted to the unassuming and mundane heroism of the defenders of the city. The new emperor who wept over *Childhood* read the story and immediately ordered that Tolstoy be transferred to a less dangerous place. He believed that 'the intellectual glory of his country' required 'keeping an eye on the life of this young man'.[4] The emperor must have been less thrilled by the later Sebastopol stories. 'Sebastopol in May', mauled by the censors, witnessed the birth of a passionate pacifism that would later become one of the pillars of Tolstoy's worldview along with a growing understanding of the utter futility of sacrifices made by the Russian people. The author ended the story with the telling observation that his only 'ever beautiful hero' (*cw*, IV, p. 59) was truth. In 'Sebastopol in August' Tolstoy described the final assault of the French army and the death of the main character, the young, charming and naively patriotic sub-officer who bravely and uselessly did not leave the trenches as the enemy advanced. 'Something in a greatcoat was lying at the place, where Volodya stood' (*cw*, IV, p. 116), the narrator wryly remarks. The story ends with the powerless fury of Russian soldiers leaving the city they had selflessly defended for eleven months.

Tolstoy was a brave and diligent, but not very disciplined officer. One of his peers later remembered that he used to leave his brigade without permission on quiet days to participate in clashes elsewhere and he constantly argued with superiors. After the fall of Sebastopol Tolstoy decided that a military career was not for him. The Sebastopol stories turned a young and promising beginner into the acknowledged leader of Russian literature and, by default, public opinion. Literature was to become 'his chief and only occupation'. He also aspired to 'literary fame' (*Ds*, p. 93). Like Thackeray, whom he admired, Tolstoy saw in vanity a powerful engine of human behaviour 'even among the people ready to die for their principles' (*cw*, IV, p. 24), but described this human weakness without the indignation of the British satirist. Now he had plenty of opportunities to satisfy his own vanity.

In the autumn of 1855 Tolstoy was granted leave and left his brigade and military service forever. On his way to St Petersburg he confessed in his diary that 'sexuality torments him' (*Ds*, p. 93) and repented for having gambled away an exorbitant amount of money. To repay at least part of the debt, he asked his brother to sell the mansion at Yasnaya Polyana, in which he had been born. The house was disassembled and moved to a neighbouring estate. For the remaining 55 years of his life, Tolstoy had to live in one of the two remaining wings of the building.

Tolstoy both enjoyed and loathed his new-found celebrity. In St Petersburg he was welcomed in the most exclusive literary circles and aristocratic salons. Turgenev, the doyen of Russian literature, invited Tolstoy to stay at his house and was ready to go to Yasnaya Polyana to introduce himself. Willing to acclaim this new genius and recognize his pre-eminence, Turgenev nonetheless wanted to guide his younger colleague, believing that this rough diamond needed polish. Tolstoy, however, was the last person to accept any sort of patronage. He was always ready to argue against received wisdom, especially when pronounced by important people and in an authoritative manner. George Sand was worshipped by Russian radicals for her powerful defence of gender equality, but memoirists recall Tolstoy arguing that her female heroines, if they really existed,

Tolstoy's house in Yasnaya Polyana.

should be dragged along the streets of St Petersburg. Another time he insisted that only a man who had imbibed pompous nonsense could admire Homer and Shakespeare. Still, these provocative statements represented minor eccentricities compared with his categorical denial that literary people surrounding him in St Petersburg had any convictions at all.

The contributors to *Sovremennik*, gathering at Nekrasov's house, were incensed, certain not only of the firmness of their convictions, but that these mattered for the future of Russia:

> 'Why then do you come to us', said Turgenev in a choking high voice (which always happened during passionate debates), recalls a memoirist. 'You don't belong here. Go to princess Belosel'skaia-Belozerskaia!'
>
> 'Why should I ask you where to go!' Tolstoy replied.
> 'And even if I leave, the idle talk won't turn into convictions.'[5]

For Tolstoy convictions were not a matter for intellectual debates or political articles, but a question of life and death; one should be ready to die for them. He was eager to show his new friends that he preferred not only high society but outright debauchery to literary conversations. As usual, he would afterwards reproach himself for wasting his life so uselessly and foolishly:

> We went to Pavlovsk. Disgusting! Wenches. Stupid
> music, wenches, an artificial nightingale, wenches,
> heat, cigarette smoke, wenches, vodka, cheese, wild
> shrieks, wenches, wenches, wenches! Everyone tried to
> pretend they were enjoying themselves, and they liked
> the wenches, but without success. (*Ds*, p. 101).

For a while St Petersburg writers were ready to tolerate Tolstoy's insolence and dissipated way of life out of respect for his genius. A romance between Tolstoy's married sister and Turgenev did not help relations with the latter, which continued under strain before finally breaking down in 1861. The quarrel lasted for seventeen years and ended only in 1878 in a touching, if somewhat half-hearted, reconciliation.

Another literary acquaintance that Tolstoy made in St Petersburg soon developed into a lifetime friendship. Afanasii Fet, one of Russia's finest lyrical poets, who described in his memoirs Tolstoy's quarrels with Turgenev, was the adopted son of a provincial landowner, Afanasii Shenshin. In a bout of passion, the elder Shenshin had abducted a young German woman, Scharlotta Fet, from her first husband when she was already pregnant. Fet's close friends including Tolstoy believed that his parents were of Jewish origin. Defying all marital laws, Shenshin contrived to marry Scharlotta, but fourteen years later the forgery was discovered and he had to disinherit the boy, depriving him of noble status, property and even his surname. Deeply traumatized, Fet for many years desperately tried to regain his lost name and social position, initially through military service and then with the help of a loveless marriage of convention and skilful estate management. To achieve these goals he abandoned Maria Lazich, the greatest love of his life, who was hopelessly poor. Tragically, Maria died shortly afterwards (we shall never know whether it was an accident or suicide). At the same time Fet wrote poems full of passionate and tender love for this world coupled with a no less powerful longing for the other. Tolstoy could appreciate this odd combination of poetical madness and militant rationality like no one else. However, he never was able or wanted to take both these qualities apart and to confine them to separate spheres of his life. Already in St Petersburg he was envisaging for himself a new social role.

In March 1856 Alexander II told representatives of the Moscow nobility that the abolition of serfdom was inevitable and needed to be implemented from above before the peasants started to liberate themselves by force. The reform would require Herculean efforts. Land in Russia was owned by the nobles, thus transferring it to peasants would amount to an outright confiscation of property, while liberating serfs without land would immediately create millions of rural poor in a state that lacked a bureaucratic infrastructure that could cope with them. The emperor created a secret commission to deal with the issue, but at the same time urged nobles to take the initiative and settle the issue themselves on their own estates.

In May 1856, equally fed up with writers, wenches and aristocrats, Tolstoy went to Yasnaya Polyana to become a model emancipator. He drafted his plan of liberation and hoped to create a solution that could be replicated by many others. Unfortunately, the peasants were unable to believe that a landowner could offer them an honest deal. They expected a better arrangement from the tsar whom they still trusted. Tolstoy, who was sure that his settlement plan was much more generous than anything the crown would ever be able or willing to offer, was frustrated and incensed. The bitter experience of this miscommunication is evoked in his

The writers of *Sovremennik*: Tolstoy standing on the left, Turgenev sitting second left, 1856.

story 'The Morning of a Landowner'. The young noble protagonist spends the day trying to alleviate the misery of his peasants and ends it with a 'mixed feeling of tiredness, shame, powerlessness and repentance' (*CW*, IV, p. 167).

On 10 January 1857 Tolstoy received a passport and, for the first time in his life, went abroad. He travelled first to Paris, the acknowledged cultural capital of Europe. After staying there for two months, Tolstoy suddenly left 'for moral reasons' and rushed to Switzerland to see the landscapes glorified by Rousseau. There he also met his good friend and second cousin once removed, Alexandra Tolstoy, lady-in-waiting to the new empress. Tolstoy had enjoyed visiting Paris theatres and concerts, but his general impressions were negative. He was especially repulsed by and could never forget a public execution he had witnessed. The self-confident and unabashed sexual licence also created an unfavourable impression on him. Alexandra recalled that the first thing her cousin told her was that in the *pension* where he lived nineteen couples out of 36 (that is, slightly over half) were unmarried (*LNT & AAT*, p. 12). One can probably doubt the figures – Tolstoy could hardly have been able to perform an exhaustive sociological survey – but the emotion was genuine. These reactions require an explanation. Why should a man who has witnessed hundreds of deaths on the battlefield be so profoundly shocked by the execution of a convicted murderer? Why was a regular customer of brothels so easily scandalized by mere cohabitation?

Both feelings, however, had the same roots. In a letter from Paris to the critic Vasily Botkin, Tolstoy wrote that he had seen 'many horrible things in war . . . but if a man had been torn to pieces before my eyes, it would not have been so revolting as this ingenious and elegant machine by means of which a strong, hale and hearty man was killed in an instant' (*Ls*, i, p. 95). It was the formal, procedural character of the killing that he found so disgusting. In the same way, he was accustomed to struggles with his own sexuality and to succumbing to lust, which caused him 'physical pain'. He could not, however, reconcile himself with what he regarded as normalized vice that was completely content with itself. He could clearly see the first manifestations of an impersonal modern state so different from the despotism and arbitrariness of Russia, and he did not like it. The stay in Paris strongly contributed to Tolstoy's anarchistic ideology. In the same letter to Botkin, he claimed that 'any state is a conspiracy designed not only to exploit, but above all to corrupt its citizens' (*Ls*, i, pp. 95–6) and that he believed in moral, religious and artistic laws that were not mandatory, but not in political ones.

In many respects, this attitude amounted to a total refutation of modernity. In a letter to Turgenev from Switzerland, Tolstoy pleaded with him not to use the railway, which compared to travelling in a carriage was like a brothel compared to love: 'convenient, but also inhumanly mechanical and deadly monotonous' (*Ls*, i, p. 97). He enjoyed walks in the Swiss mountains for the whole summer and planned to continue his Grand Tour to Germany and Italy. Then, in July, he lost all his money at roulette in Baden-Baden and had to cut short his trip. He returned to 'delightful Yasnaya' and 'disgusting Russia' with its 'coarse and deceitful life' (*Ds*, p. 127). In a letter to Alexandra Tolstoy he complained about the 'patriarchal barbarism, thievery and lawlessness' (*Ls*, i, p. 63) of his motherland.

Tolstoy blamed the government for this disastrous state of affairs. For too long it had ignored the overwhelming majority of the nation. Now, cynically or stupidly, it was promising benefits that could never be delivered. In a speech in 1858 the emperor reproached the nobility for sabotaging the reform. In response, Tolstoy drafted a memo arguing that the liberation of the serfs had been the historic dream of the nobility, the only estate that had sent its 'martyrs in 25 and 48 to exile and the gallows'. He ended the note by claiming that 'if, God forbid, the fire of peasant rebellion, with which the tsar was threatening landowners, were ever to break out, the best thing it could do would be to destroy the government' (*cw*, v, pp. 268, 270). In a unique display of caution, Tolstoy burned the memorandum 'without showing it to anyone' (*Ds*, p. 136).

Tolstoy searched for ways to take Russia out of patriarchal barbarity without submitting it to the 'inhumanly mechanistic' forces of modern civilization. He still believed that the only way to achieve this was to establish some sort of rapprochement between the educated nobles and the peasants, the only two social classes that lived on the land. He started freeing his serfs, but placed his hopes not in the imminent reform, but in educating future generations. Tolstoy started a school for peasant children in one of the two remaining wings of his house. He felt he needed to learn more about current pedagogical practice so, in the summer of 1860, he left the school to the supervision of his assistant and went abroad to study the experiments in primary education. Tolstoy wanted his school to serve as a national model. Upon his return he resumed teaching, but also inaugurated twenty other schools in the neighbouring villages. He founded the pedagogical magazine *Yasnaya Polyana* and tried to create a National Society for Education.

Tolstoy devised his own pedagogical system based as much on Rousseau's *Emile* as on his own ideas about human nature and the needs of peasant children. He completely abandoned the strict discipline prevalent in nineteenth-century schools and never asked pupils to memorize texts by heart, study calligraphy or learn difficult rules. His school barely had any curriculum at all, instead he relied on free communication between teacher and pupils, engaged children in conversations, joint physical work and physical exercises. He read them books, told stories based on events from Russian history, including the Napoleonic wars, and his own rich and varied experience. The basic sciences were often taught out of the classroom through direct observations of nature. Peasant children were often needed for different sorts of work at home and were free to leave school whenever necessary. Tolstoy wanted to teach his pupils only the things that had practical or moral importance. Corporal punishment, which was the usual practice of the time, was completely forbidden. The school was also open to girls.

Pupils were more than enthusiastic. Tolstoy's teaching methods could doubtfully be replicated elsewhere, but such a passionate, charismatic and dedicated teacher and the immediate associates he had personally trained could achieve a lot. In 1862 Tolstoy published his famous article 'Who should learn how to write from whom – peasant children from us or we from the peasant children?' He expressed admiration for the instinctive creative genius and learning abilities of his pupils. There was, however, less humility on Tolstoy's part than the title of the article suggested. The process of learning was mutual. To produce writing of such artlessness and simplicity that the great writer was eager to emulate, the peasant children had first to acquire from him not only basic literacy, but the power of imagination, intellectual curiosity and a desire to express themselves. This was exactly the type of communication and trust that Tolstoy the emancipator failed to build with their parents. In one of his pedagogical conversations with his pupils he half jokingly, half seriously, discussed his own wish to renounce his status of a landowner and to start working on the land. Initially incredulous, the children finally started believing their teacher really meant it.

Fascinated by the idea of a miraculous transformation of a *barin* (landowner) into a *muzhik* (peasant), children began discussing the prospect of Tolstoy marrying a peasant girl. They understood well that such an outrageous change of social status implied an equally improbable family arrangement. Tolstoy readily engaged in this ridiculous discussion. He was 'smiling, asking questions, writing something in his notebook'[6] and obviously learning from peasant children 'how to write'. The whole story they were collectively conceiving was strikingly close to some of his literary designs.

Since 1853 Tolstoy had constantly been returning to a story, later known as *The Cossacks*, dedicated to the part of his life he had not yet transformed into artistic work. The plot was typical of Romantic colonial literature: a young aristocratic officer, whose name Tolstoy changed several times, disappointed with the shallow life of high society, falls in love with a beautiful Cossack girl, or in some versions, a married woman, whose name, Marianna, did not change from the first draft to the last. Tolstoy presents this strong and blatantly erotic passion as an expression of his character's desire to change his life forever and share the simple, violent and natural life of a Cossack. The outcome of this endeavour was not clear to the author: in some versions the officer fell out of love with Marianna after seducing her, in others he happily married her. Tolstoy was also experimenting with the language, contrasting the sophisticated psychologically nuanced style of the officer's letters to his friend in St Petersburg with the particularity and directness of Cossack speech.

In parallel with his work on *The Cossacks*, Tolstoy was also working on an idyllic epic about peasant life in mainland Russia that also revolved around a powerful and sexually attractive woman. The language in these unfinished stories or fragments, provisionally entitled *The Idyll* and *Tikhon and Malanya*, is much more thoroughly stylized than in the drafts of *The Cossacks*, since there is no repentant noble to serve as a narrator. Nevertheless, Tolstoy's loving and idealizing gaze can be perceived in the way he exoticizes peasant life with the detached admiration of an outsider.

These drafts evoke one of the strongest erotic infatuations of Tolstoy's life, his affair with a married peasant, Aksinya Bazykina. Tolstoy regularly mentions Aksinya in his diaries for 1858–60 with the usual admixture of frenzied desire and revulsion, but the entries also record a fixation on the same person that was much less usual. Thirty years later, in a completely different period of his life, he recalled this passion in a story with a revealing title, 'The Devil'. This emotional colouring was clearly present in the affair from the very beginning, but at the same time Tolstoy recorded different feelings in his diary:

> I am a fool. A beast. Her neck is red with the sun . . . I am in love as never before in my life. I've no other thoughts. I am tormented . . . Had Aksinya, but I am repelled by her . . . Aksinya I recall only with revulsion – her shoulders . . . Continue to see Aksinya exclusively . . . She was nowhere about. I looked for her. It's no longer the feeling of a stag, but of a husband for a wife. It's strange. I try to reawaken my former feeling of surfeit and I can't. (*Ds*, pp. 134–5, 139; *cw*, XLVIII, p. 25)

Tolstoy's female characters based on Aksinya totally lack a satanic dimension. Both Malanya and Marianna are inherently chaste, in spite of their sex appeal, liveliness and playfulness. Their seductive power is morally redeemed because it is rooted in the primordial simplicity of the world the author longed to join.

In any case, Tolstoy was unable to complete these works. His preoccupation with taking writing lessons from peasant children betrayed deep dissatisfaction with the course of his own literary activity. He regarded all his new stories like 'Albert' and 'Lucerne', discussing the inevitable misery and loneliness of a true artist, or the moralistic tale 'Three Deaths', or 'Family Happiness', where a young woman recalls her romance, conflict and reconciliation with her husband, as outright failures and even 'abominations' that he only sent to the magazines for economic reasons. After 'Family Happiness' appeared in 1859 he stopped publishing and did his best to conceal from his literary friends that he was writing at all.

Friends, publishers and critics were desperate. Both Turgenev and Fet urged him to resume writing. Nekrasov tried to convince him that he possessed everything needed to write 'good – simple, calm and clear stories', not understanding that this is exactly what Tolstoy was reluctant to do. When the critic Alexander Druzhinin, who published the magazine *Biblioteka dlia chtenia* (Library for Reading), asked Tolstoy for new prose for his magazine, Tolstoy responded that he lacked 'the content' that 'demands to be released and gives audacity, pride and power' (*TP*, I, p. 289). He felt ashamed at the age of 31 'to write stories, which are very nice and pleasant to read' (*Ls*, I, p. 129). He left Russia in 1860, insisting that he had renounced literature and was interested only in methods for teaching in popular schools. However, during this second 'educational' trip he started to believe that he had finally discovered the content that he needed.

The rapid changes in the social fabric of Europe that were taking place in the nineteenth century dramatically increased the demand for formal education. An individual could no longer assume he would lead the same life as his parents. The children of the working classes could not rely on the practical training they received from their families. New types of schools were proliferating and new pedagogical ideas being tested. Tolstoy, who was convinced that teaching was his lifelong vocation, was anxious to get first-hand information on the process. The practices he observed left him profoundly disappointed since the European schools he visited were using the same disciplinary practices he loathed at home.

He had another much more personal and traumatic reason for the trip. His eldest brother Nikolai, who since their childhood had served as a guide, mentor and role model for the young Leo, was slowly dying from consumption and the doctors demanded a change of climate. They went initially to the German resort of Bad Soden and then to the south of France, accompanied by their sister Maria and her children. Maria had her share of troubles, her marriage collapsed and her relations with Turgenev went nowhere.

Tolstoy had witnessed people dying and had lost loved ones, but this time he had to experience both. His brother Dmitry also died from consumption in 1856, but Leo was not present at his deathbed and Dmitry never was as close to him as Nikolai. Three weeks after Nikolai's death Tolstoy wrote to Fet that, while everyone was amazed how quietly his brother had passed away, he was the only one to understand how excruciating it was, as not a single one of the dying man's feelings had escaped him:

> He did not say that he felt the death approaching, but I know he followed its every step and surely knew what still remained to him of life. A few minutes before he died, he dozed off, then suddenly came to and whispered in horror: 'why, what is that?' He had seen it – this absorption of the self in nothingness. (*Ls*, I, p. 141)

The presence of death turned life into an agonizing wait. Tolstoy had acutely felt, perhaps as never before, the pointlessness of existence. At the same time he was fascinated by the mystery of death. In his letter to Sergei, his only brother still alive, he recorded the astonishing impression of beauty and calm on the face of their dead brother released from the terrible suffering of his final days.

From the south of France Tolstoy went to Rome and Florence. Italy had been on the itinerary of his 1857 tour, but he had failed to make it there because of self-inflicted financial problems. In 1860 he was drawn to Italy not so much by its tourist attractions, but by his desire to meet Prince Sergei Volkonsky, a distant relative and a former Decembrist. The 'martyrs of 1825', who had sacrificed their privileged positions, families and properties to liberate the serfs, interested Tolstoy through his entire life. In 1895, when the famous painter Ilya Repin asked him to suggest a theme for a historical painting, Tolstoy suggested the five leaders of the uprising being led to the gallows. After Alexander II granted amnesty to the Decembrists in 1856, he began to contemplate a story or novel about them.

One could barely imagine a historical character better suited to Tolstoy's interests than Volkonsky. A rich aristocrat who owned more than 2,000 serfs, a decorated hero of the Napoleonic wars and a full general, Volkonsky had renounced his dissipated way of life to join the Decembrist conspiracy. Shortly before his arrest he had married Maria Raevskaya, a renowned beauty celebrated by Pushkin, who then followed her husband to Siberia. Having served nearly ten years of hard labour, Volkonsky settled in a remote village where he became a highly successful farmer on the land allotted to him. Later allowed to live in the provincial city of Irkutsk, he preferred the company of merchants and peasants to local high society. He was also deeply eccentric and prone to passionate mystic religiosity.

Trying to recover from the depression that overcame him after Nikolai's death, Tolstoy started to work on *The Decembrists*, a novel describing the return of an amnestied exile to Moscow in 1856 with his wife and two children. He wanted to contrast the moral vigour of an old man who had experienced terrible hardships with the vanity of

Moscow liberal salons, with their empty talk about the problems of the day. He wanted to write about people who remained loyal to their convictions in the face of adversity and proved it with their lives. Both psychologically and linguistically, it was easier for Tolstoy to identify with an old eccentric aristocrat than with peasants or Cossacks. On 16 October 1860, one month after Nikolai's death, Tolstoy wrote in his diary, 'The one way to live is to work' (*Ds*, p. 142). A month or two later he met Volkonsky and by February 1861 he was able to read three draft chapters of his novel to Turgenev in Paris.

Pleased to see Tolstoy returning to literature, Turgenev enjoyed the chapters. Most likely, he did not see that the new work was directed against him and his literary environment. Three months later, when the two writers met at Fet's house in Russia, Turgenev proudly told his friends that his natural daughter herself repaired the clothing of beggars. Tolstoy chose not to conceal that he found this repulsive and theatrical. Turgenev promised to 'punch him in the face' (*Ls*, I, p. 150). The quarrel ended with a formal challenge to a duel that, happily for Russian literature, never took place. Relations between the writers, however, were broken, as Tolstoy wrote to Fet in January 1862: 'Turgenev is a scoundrel who needs thrashing' (*Ls*, I, p. 152).

Before heading to Russia, Tolstoy visited London and Brussels. In London he conversed with the political exile and revolutionary thinker Alexander Herzen, who was editing the newspaper *Bell* and the magazine *Polar Star*, which were smuggled into Russia. The title *Polar Star* was taken from the Decembrist almanac of the 1820s. In it, Herzen published a great deal of historical material about the Decembrists and chapters from his huge autobiography *My Past and Thoughts*, where he claimed that his political awakening happened when, at thirteen years old in 1826, he had for the first time heard about the rebels and made the oath to revenge them.

Tolstoy's political views were different from Herzen's. Their perception of the Decembrists also differed a lot, but the fascination with the heroic self-sacrifice was equally strong. Tolstoy intended to discuss his future novel with the famous exile, but for unknown reasons, never did. He only wrote about his novel in a letter to Herzen sent from Brussels on 14 March 1861. In the same letter, Tolstoy asked whether Herzen had already read the proclamation abolishing serfdom that had finally been issued in Russia on 19 February 1861. Produced after five years of fierce debates, feuds and conflicts among different high-ranking courtiers and bureaucrats, clans and interest groups, this was a muddled compromise. Tolstoy was predictably disappointed. As he put it, 'the peasants won't understand a word, and we won't believe a word' (*Ls*, I, p. 145). Still, he could not fail to grasp that the world around him had irrevocably changed.

Tensions in the literary world were already running high before the proclamation. In the late 1850s the leading writers affiliated to *Sovremennik* had left the magazine, led by Turgenev, because they were dismayed by the powerful position that had been gained by the magazine's in-house critics, Nikolai Chernyshevsky and Nikolai Dobroliubov. These sons of priests, former seminarians, militant atheists and political radicals were challenging the long-established monopoly of the educated liberal nobility in Russian social, cultural and literary life. Nekrasov, a noble himself, took the part of the critics both because of his political sympathies and an astute understanding of the market. In a time of turmoil and loosening of censorship, the direct statements of *Sovremennik*'s critics defined the spirit of the magazine and excited the readers even more than the most exquisite novels.

Tolstoy had severed his exclusive publishing agreement with *Sovremennik* earlier. When he entered the literary world, Chernyshevsky had welcomed *Youth* and *Boyhood* for their subtlety of psychological analysis and coined the term 'dialectics of the soul', which became a catchword for Tolstoy's style. Still, his attitude to Tolstoy betrayed the condescending arrogance of a hard-working professional intellectual towards an aristocratic dilettante. Tolstoy's reaction was equally arrogant, but much more emotional. In one of his letters to Nekrasov, he called Chernyshevsky a 'gentleman who smells of lice' (*Ls*, I, p. 59). At the same time, his attitude towards noble liberals was hardly more generous. Their compassion for the plight of the poor seemed to him like the mending of a beggar's clothes by an elegant noble girl under the guidance of an English governess. Returning to Russia in the aftermath of the liberation of serfs, he felt it necessary to settle scores.

Tolstoy's reputation as a raw genius, together with his insatiable intellectual curiosity, provoked many highly intelligent people to try to educate him. In the 1850s Boris Chicherin, the prominent historian and legal thinker, was arguably the most powerful mind to take on this impossible task. In a letter to Tolstoy written in April 1861, Chicherin declared that he was finishing an article about the abolition of serfdom and chided Tolstoy for hiding himself from the major problems of his time behind the petty preoccupations of teaching illiterate children. On his way home, Tolstoy responded from Dresden:

> You regard convictions acquired not by meticulously following a course, but through the sufferings of the whole life and the most passionate quest for truth that is possible for a human being, as the exaltation of self-love and paucity of thought . . . You find it strange to teach dirty children. I can't understand how someone, if he respects himself, can write an article. Can you say in an article one millionth of what you know and what should be said, or anything new, or any thought that would be just, truly just. (*CW*, LX, p. 380)

Whatever one thinks about Tolstoy's pedagogical pursuits, they were highly successful. In the country, where peasants were almost universally illiterate, their children did not have much choice. The peasants anticipating the coming changes were eager to send their children to schools. The rapidly multiplying numbers of young graduates were willing to teach and the pupils were interested in learning. Tolstoy brought to this enterprise his usual diligence and energy. Having issued the first edition of his magazine *Yasnaya Polyana*, he wrote a letter to Chernyshevsky asking him to review it in *Sovremennik*, wanting to disseminate his ideas among the readers of the hugely more popular publication.

Chernyshevsky reacted in an article written with his characteristic sense of papal infallibility. He praised Tolstoy for his good intentions, but was profoundly sceptical about the usefulness of such an unsystematic way of teaching. Tolstoy claimed that the educated people do not understand what lower classes need and thus can have no idea what and how to teach them. In response, Chernyshevsky advised him to go first to university and find out what every teacher needed to know.

Conservatives were no less appalled by what they regarded as a dangerous effort to bring millions of people out from under the control of the establishment during one of the most turbulent periods of Russian history. For several months Tolstoy served in the newly instituted role of civic arbiter, trying to reconcile the interests of the landowners and peasants in the conflicts that were inevitably emerging as the process of reform was being implemented. He coped with this far less well than he had as a teacher. The peasants usually obstinately refused to hear his arguments, which they probably could not understand, while the nobles hated him intensely. In April 1862 Tolstoy resigned from the office citing health reasons. He also started to feel that he could not fully devote himself to his teaching duties.

The letter to Chicherin shows Tolstoy's preoccupation not only with teaching, but with the question of what actually could or could not be said in words, and what kind of words can express truth. In his magazine, Tolstoy recorded conversations with children about the meaning of art, about the nature of the state and the law, about Russian history and the Napoleonic wars. These descriptions of the opening of young minds to the complexity of the world, their inherent wisdom and inquisitiveness, their different characters and changing attitude to the knowledge they acquired are among the very best pages written by Tolstoy, at least before he started work on his great novels. Knowing Tolstoy's characteristic blend of documentary effect and artistic idealization, one can only wonder what was actually happening during these lessons.

He was again full of literary plans. During his European journey he wrote 'Polikushka', a morbid story about the recruit draft in a village, the destructive force of money and the immense evil produced by a self-righteous and sentimental landlady who believes she is entitled to improve the morality of her peasants. Tolstoy was also working on *The Decembrists*, *The Cossacks* and the village idyll *Tikhon and Malanya*. The tide of literary inspiration was on the rise, but drafts were lying uselessly in his drawer and new plans were tormenting his mind. At the same time he was teaching children, hiring students, propagating new teaching methods and had managed to convince everyone around, and most importantly, himself, that he had discovered his true path in teaching. Tolstoy faced an extremely difficult choice. History, as usual taking the side of the winner, intervened to help him.

The years immediately after the abolition of serfdom were tumultuous. Many villages around Russia saw disjointed but violent rebellions by peasants who believed that the nobles were concealing from them the actual will of the tsar. The atmosphere in the capital was also tense and the radical movement was growing. In May 1862 a series of powerful fires, believed to be the result of arson, broke out in St Petersburg. The government started an investigation and a wave of new arrests. In June Chernyshevsky was arrested for instigating a peasant uprising and *Sovremennik* was temporarily closed. On 6 July 1862 Tolstoy's estate in Yasnaya Polyana was searched by the secret police following entirely false accusations that he was keeping an illegal printing press. Nothing suspicious was found, but in the process the police turned the house and the whole village upside down, looked in the barn and the pond, scared his old aunt Toinette and his sister Maria to death and, most outrageously, read Tolstoy's intimate diary and correspondence.

Tolstoy was absent from Yasnaya Polyana when the secret police came. Having lost two brothers to consumption, he had become anxious about his own health and travelled to the Bashkir villages on the Volga to drink *kumys*, the horse milk popular among the locals, which was believed to have healing effects. He received the news about the raid on his way back and felt himself insulted as an aristocrat, an anarchist and a Russian patriot who devoted his life to healing social divisions instead of inflaming them – and first and foremost as a human being. 'How extraordinarily lucky it was, that I wasn't there', he wrote to Alexandra Tolstoy, 'if I had been, I should probably be on trial for murder by now.'

The school could not continue. For a while Tolstoy considered 'expatriating'. He reassured his cousin that he would not join Herzen and get engaged in his subversive activities:

Herzen has his way and I have mine. Nor shall I hide. I shall loudly proclaim that I am selling my estate in order to leave Russia, where it is impossible to know a minute in advance that they won't chain you up or flog you together with your sister, your wife, and your mother – I am going away. (*Ls*, i, pp. 162, 160)

He did not go into self-imposed exile and actually never again left Russia, not even temporarily. The catastrophe relieved him of his obligations and set him free to follow his calling. Tolstoy was certain that to be able to produce work that would finally satisfy him, he needed to change his lifestyle completely. The only way to achieve this radical transformation, he knew, was to get married.

2

A Married Genius

The thought of marriage was not new to Tolstoy. From his early twenties he had been envisaging the idea of family life. When he arrived in Moscow in 1851, he set himself three aims: '1) to gamble, 2) to marry, 3) to obtain a post' (*Ds*, p. 19). He managed only the first. Five years later, he confided to his diary an intention 'to go to the country' and 'get married as soon as possible' (*Ds*, p. 99). On 1 January 1859 he made another New Year's resolution: 'must marry this year or not at all' (*Ds*, p. 138). As his diaries and letters reveal, over the years he had considered nearly a dozen young women as prospective brides. Only once, however, did Tolstoy take practical steps in this direction. In 1856 he planned to marry Valeria Arsenieva, the orphaned daughter of some country neighbours, for whom Tolstoy was acting as guardian.

Tolstoy's courtship proceeded in a predictably tortured manner. He constantly questioned himself in his diary whether he loved Valeria and whether she was capable of true love. One day he found her attractive and sweet, another repugnant and stupid. He also bombarded the girl with long didactic letters telling her how she should dress, behave and feel in order to become a good wife. Their frequent conversations doubtless evolved on similar lines. Both parties eventually tired of such peculiar relations. After half a year of hopeless deliberations, Tolstoy suddenly went abroad sending Valeria a formal apology. Two years later, an idealized version of Valeria, as he imagined her at the height of his self-imposed infatuation, appeared in Tolstoy's *Family Happiness*, a novella that described life as it might have been if he and Valeria were married.

'While education is free, upbringing is based on coercion,' Tolstoy wrote a couple of years later in his article 'Upbringing and Education'. 'There is no right to an upbringing. I do not recognize this right. The young generation that always and everywhere protests against the coercion of upbringing does not recognize it, has never recognized it and never will' (*cw*, VIII, pp. 215–16). Meanwhile, it was precisely this type of coercive upbringing that Tolstoy practised on poor Valeria, while she dared not protest for fear of losing such an enviable match. In fact, Tolstoy never regarded the family as a union of two separate human beings, but rather as a joint symbiotic personality. In *Anna Karenina* Konstantin Levin is surprised to find out that his wife became for him an integral part of his own self and he 'could not now tell where she ended and he began' (*AK*, p. 438). Tolstoy's vision of family happiness was as maximalist and uncompromising as was his notion of literary perfection. Yet he also realized that if he failed at marriage he would not be given a second chance.

> Before falling in love with his future wife, Levin often visited the Shcherbatskys and fell in love with the family. Strange as it may seem, it was the whole Shcherbatsky family – especially the feminine part of it – that Levin was in love with. He could not remember his mother . . . so that in the Scherbatskys' house he saw family life for the first time . . . such as he had been deprived of by the death of his own father and mother. All the members of that family, especially the women, appeared to him as though wrapped in some mystic poetic veil, and he not only saw no defects in them, but imagined behind that poetic veil the loftiest feelings and every possible perfection. (*AK*, p. 19)

The marriage of the two elder Shcherbatsky sisters relieved Levin of the necessity to choose. Tolstoy's relationship with the family of the doctor Andrei Bers was similar, but more complicated. Andrei's wife Liubov', born Islavina, is described in *Childhood*. As rumours had it, as a ten-year-old Lev had once pushed her from a balcony, jealous of the attention she gave to another boy. As a friend and regular guest of the Berses, Tolstoy was captivated by the vision of family happiness he had been deprived of in his own early years: he once told his sister that if he were ever to marry, it would be to someone in the Bers family.

Andrei and Liubov' had five sons and three daughters. Tolstoy loved to spend time with the teenage girls and even played leapfrog with them. The sisters, all of whom had developed literary interests, admired 'the count' ('le comte') as they called him among themselves. Unlike Levin, his future novelistic alter ego, Tolstoy also had the allure of being a famous writer. In Russian families it was traditional to marry off daughters in order of age. When the Berses first detected Tolstoy's matrimonial intentions, they were confident that he was interested in nineteen-year-old Liza (Elizaveta), the most serious and well behaved of their daughters, whom they believed to be better prepared for matrimony than her younger siblings.

Tolstoy also was considering this possibility: 'Liza Bers tempts me, but nothing will come of it' (*Ds*, p. 145), he wrote in his diary in September 1861. Next year events took a sudden and dramatic turn. On his way to the Samara steppes for a course of *kumys* treatment, Tolstoy stayed with the Berses for a day. After his departure, the youngest sister, Tanya (Tatiana), found the middle one, Sonya (Sofia), in tears. 'Do you love the count?' asked a surprised Tanya, well known for her ability to ask awkward questions. 'I don't know,' answered Sonya, sobbing. 'His two brothers died from consumption' (*Kuz*, p. 89). Sonya had already promised her heart to a student, Mitrofan Polivanov, and fifteen-year-old Tanya, as she

Sisters Sofia (Sonya) and Tatiana (Tanya) Bers in 1861.

recalled many decades later, was struck by a sudden realization of the inherent duality of human feelings. After 'the count' returned from Samara the Berses paid two short visits to Yasnaya Polyana, where Tolstoy first took notice of Sonya not so much as a little girl, but as a charming young woman. By the time he reached Moscow in August 1862, Tolstoy was already asking himself the perennial question: did the feelings he was experiencing amount to real love? 'I am afraid for myself – what if this is only the desire for love, and not love? I try to look only at her weak sides, but still. A child! It could be' (*Ds*, p. 146).

In the short and tumultuous romance that rapidly started to unfold between a 34-year-old man with rich and varied experience and an innocent girl of eighteen, Sonya took a definite lead. Already in August she was telling Tolstoy that she had written a story describing the complex situation in the family. As her younger sister recalled, the story had two characters: the middle-aged Prince

The *Preshpekt*, the main route to the house in Yasnaya Polyana, 1903–5.

Dublitsky, energetic and intelligent with 'unattractive appearance' and 'fickle opinions', and Smirnov, a young man of positive, calm temperament with 'lofty ideals'. The female character Elena was a young and beautiful girl with big black eyes. She had two sisters: the elder, cold Zinaida in love with Dublitsky, and the younger, lively Natasha. Smirnov fell in love with Elena, and proposed to her, but her parents were hesitant, considering the couple too young for marriage. Suddenly Elena started to realize that she loved Dublitsky, who also preferred her to her sister, and felt guilty before both Zinaida and Smirnov. At some point, exhausted by the inner conflict, Elena contemplated retiring to a convent, but finally managed to arrange a marriage between Dublitsky and Zinaida while herself marrying Smirnov.

On 26 August 1862 Sonya handed the story to Tolstoy who, as usual, was deeply unsure whether he deserved to be loved. It is difficult to imagine a more provocative move. Sofia's story made the renowned author feel encouraged, touched, excited and mortified at the same time:

She gave me a story to read. What force of truth and simplicity! The uncertainty torments her. I read it without a sinking heart, jealousy or envy, but 'unusually unattractive appearance' and 'fickleness of opinions' touched me on the raw. I am calmed down now. All this is not for me. (*Ds*, p. 146)

In his diary Tolstoy reflected further about Sonya's possible intentions, using his characteristic psychological analysis of the layered structure of human motives: 'On the way back I thought: either it is all unintentional, or her feelings are unusually subtle, or it is the basest coquetry . . . or else it's unintentional and subtle and coquettish' (*Ds*, p. 147).

In response to the story, he wrote a letter to Sonya explaining that he was misunderstood in her family and never really loved Liza or intended to marry her. Not daring to commit this explanation fully to paper, Tolstoy limited himself to using the initial letters of every word. In one of the most memorable episodes in *Anna Karenina*, Kitty, guided by the miraculous intuition of a loving woman, understands the message written to her by Levin in the same way. Whether it was the spell of Tolstoy's novel or the power of a family legend, which it reflected, Countess Sofia Tolstoy repeated the same story in her memoirs. In fact, this display of celestial harmony between like-minded souls never actually took place. In his diary Tolstoy explicitly says that Sonya 'made him decipher the letter' (*Ds*, p. 147). Regardless of this, his passion was growing stronger and stronger.

'Don't intrude where youth, poetry, beauty and love are' (*Ds*, p. 147), Tolstoy wrote in his diary on 7 September 1862. He then immediately proceeded to confess that deep in his heart he was imagining Sofia reading this entry and that he actually had made it 'for her'. Three days later he left the Bers house 'without hope and more in love than ever'. While he desperately wanted to 'cut the knot' and to 'tell her and Tanechka', Tolstoy lacked the courage to do so. By now the whole family, except for Liza, who still cherished hopes of her own, realized what was happening. 'I am beginning to hate Liza as well as pity her,' wrote Tolstoy in his diary. 'Lord help me and guide me' (*Ds*, p. 148). His frenzy became unbearable:

> I am in love, as I never believed was possible to love. I am mad, I'll shoot myself if it goes on like this. Spent the evening at their house. She is charming in every way. But I am the repulsive Dublitsky. I should have been on my guard sooner. Granted, I am Dublitsky, but love makes me beautiful. Yes, tomorrow morning I'll go to their house. There have been moments, but I did not take advantage of them. I was timid, I should simply have spoken. I just want to go back now and say everything in front of them. Lord, help me. (*Ds*, p. 149)

On 13 September Tolstoy returned to the Berses, but once again found himself unable to speak out. The next day, realizing that making an open declaration was beyond his power, he wrote a proposal to Sofia, pleading for her to consider her response 'without hurrying'. Tolstoy assured her that he would be able to bear her 'no', but 'not to be loved as a husband as much as' he loves 'would be even more terrible' for him. (*Ls*, I, pp. 108–9). He carried the letter in his pocket for two more days, feeling unable to deliver it.

There was more to Tolstoy's indecision than a usual fear of making an irreversible step, excessive shyness or even the acute sense of the burden of age and sinful experience he had to carry in his new life. He was determined that not only future family happiness, but the fulfilment of his literary calling and chances for moral salvation depended upon the choice and the power of Sofia's love and devotion to him. He found himself on the verge of either absolute bliss or eternal ruin. At some point he composed a different version of his letter, explaining why he had to renounce hope and stop visiting: 'I demand from marriage something terrible, impossible. To be loved as I can love, but this is impossible.' Then he decided to take the risk. 'My God, how afraid I am of dying,' he confessed in his diary after completing his formal written proposal. 'Happiness, and such happiness, seems to me impossible' (*Ds*, p. 149).

On 16 September Tolstoy again visited the Berses and accompanied Tanya, who had a fine soprano voice, on the piano. Sonya and Liza were listening nervously nearby. Tolstoy decided that he would hand Sonya the letter if her sister managed to hit the difficult high note at the end. Tanya performed impeccably and shortly afterwards saw Sonya rushing from the room with a piece of paper in her hands, hesitantly followed by Liza. Tanya ran downstairs to the girls' room and heard Liza shouting at Sonya, demanding that she reveal what 'the count' had written to her. 'He made me a proposal,' Sofia replied quietly. 'Refuse immediately,' cried Liza hysterically. Their mother appeared, ordered Liza to stop and told Sonya to give an immediate answer. She went back and said, 'Yes, of course.' The next day Sonya explained to a desperate Polivanov that she would not have betrayed him with anyone else, but 'one cannot help loving Lev Nikolaevich' (*Kuz*, pp. 130–34).

Traditionally the preparations for a wedding in Russian noble families would take between six and eight weeks, at the least. Tolstoy would not hear of any procrastination. For the first time in his life, he felt a strong erotic attraction to a woman of his own social standing. In his diary he recalled 'the kiss by the piano and the appearance of Satan' (*Ds*, p. 150), obviously meaning sexual arousal. Apart from that, he felt that the time to realize his family utopia had arrived. He was eager to retire to Yasnaya Polyana, enjoy marital bliss and engage in the only two activities he now found appropriate: managing the estate and writing.

His impatience notwithstanding, Tolstoy subjected Sonya's love to two highly challenging tests. Convinced that spouses should be fully transparent to each other, he gave her his diaries to read. Sonya was shocked and dismayed by the descriptions of her fiancé's lust and sexual exploits, and especially by the story of his infatuation with Aksinya Bazykina, with whom he had fathered a son. Then, unable to quell his 'doubts about her love and the thought that she is deceiving herself' (*Ds*, p. 150), Tolstoy breached all customs by visiting his bride on the morning of their wedding day and drove her to tears by inquiring whether she was completely certain she wanted to marry him.

The wedding took place on 23 September 1862, a week after the engagement and exactly a month after Tolstoy had, for the first time, mentioned Sonya in his diary as 'a child'. The couple were married in the Church of the Nativity of Our Lady in the Moscow Kremlin, where Andrei Bers resided as a local doctor. The spurned Liza and the unlucky Polivanov participated in the ceremony. According to Sofia's memoirs, the marriage was consummated in the carriage taking the newlywed couple from the church to Yasnaya Polyana. Very soon Sonya was pregnant. Their first son, Sergei, was born on 28 June 1863, followed by a daughter Tatiana in 1864, and sons Ilya and Lev in 1866 and 1869, respectively.

The Tolstoys' honeymoon and the first years of their marriage were far from idyllic. Leo's feelings proved to be even more fickle than Dublitsky's opinions. During their first night at Yasnaya Polyana, he had 'a bad dream', which he summarized in his diary in two words: 'Not her' (*Ds*, p. 150). After a month of frenzied courtship, he suddenly started to suspect that he had married the wrong woman. The next day he recorded 'unbelievable happiness'. A week later 'there was a scene' that made Tolstoy 'sad that we behave just in the same way as other people'. He wept and told Sonya she had hurt him with regard to his feelings for her. 'She is charming,' he concluded in a rather unpredictable way, 'I love her even more. But is it all genuine?' (*Ds*, p. 150). Tolstoy felt there was something unnatural in their relations. In a long letter to his sister-in-law Tanya, he jokingly described a dream in which his wife had turned into a china doll (*Ls*, I, pp. 177–9). Was this a veiled expression of erotic dissatisfaction?

The inevitable difficulties of mutual adjustment were aggravated by jealousy. Sonya, stunned by the revelations about her husband's past, was constantly expecting him to revert to his old ways. In one of the entries in her diary she expressed an ardent desire to murder Aksinya and to tear off her son's head. Leo, never fully believing he deserved the love he longed for, was traumatized by every real or imaginary token of Sofia's interest towards any young man who happened to be around. Tolstoy hardly suspected her of physical infidelity; but for him feelings mattered most and he was never completely confident about his wife's inner world.

The diaries that both spouses kept during the early period of their marriage reflect constant clashes followed by passionate reconciliations. The intense emotional regime imposed by Tolstoy demanded that they share their diaries. Sofia and Leo felt a duty to be sincere and to confess every shade of feeling, but could not avoid anticipating each other's reactions. Gradually the stream of entries slowed into a trickle and then nearly stopped. They were to resume fifteen years later with even greater intensity when, for Sofia, the diary became the main tool for settling scores and proving her case before her husband and posterity.

Sofia's situation was, of course, significantly more difficult. Unlike her husband, who enjoyed his native environment, she had grown up in the Kremlin, the literal centre of the empire. A fashionable and educated city girl had to turn herself into a rural landlady, playing cards with Tolstoy's old aunt Toinette, taking care of children and sharing a responsibility for running the estate. 'He disgusts me with his peasants' (*SAT-DS*, p. 43), she confessed in her diaries two months after the marriage. Still, Sofia coped remarkably well in the circumstances. During the final months of her first pregnancy Sofia informed her younger sister that she and Lev were 'becoming real farmers and buying cattle, birds, piglets,

Tolstoy in 1862, before marriage.

calves' (*SAT-DS*, p. 526). They had also acquired 'a lot of bees' and the estate abounded with honey. During a visit to the Tolstoys Afanasy Fet was enchanted by the sight of an unexpectedly young and visibly pregnant girl running around the farm with a huge bundle of keys on her belly.

Tolstoy immersed himself in agriculture with his usual fervour. He had early decided to get rid of the stewards and managers. He did not need any intermediaries between himself and the peasants. Contrary to the persistent advice of his father-in-law, he adamantly refused to hire a steward, believing that together with Sofia they could do the job much better. On 3 May 1863 Tolstoy informed Fet that:

Sofia in 1862, before marriage.

Sonya is working with me too. We have no steward; I have people to help with the fieldwork and the building, but she manages the office and cash by herself. I have bees, sheep, a new orchard and a distillery. Everything progresses little by little, although of course poorly, compared with the ideal. (*CW*, LXI, p. 17)

Fet, who unlike his friend ran his estate as a profitable business, was unconvinced. When he asked for his sincere regards to be passed on to the countess if she was not busy 'playing dolls, sorry playing cash' (*TP*, I, p. 366), Tolstoy replied curtly:

My wife is not playing dolls at all. Do not offend her.
She seriously helps me, carrying a burden, from which
she hopes to free herself in the beginning of July. I made
a discovery . . . Try to fire all the administration and
sleep until 10, everything will go no worse. I made this
experiment and am quite satisfied with it. (*cw*, LXI, p. 20)

The abolition of serfdom had cut the traditional bond of personal
dependence between the masters and the servants. As Nekrasov,
Tolstoy's first publisher, wrote in his poem 'Who Lives Well in
Russia', 'the great chain has broken and struck the landlord by one
end and the peasant by the other.'[1] This ancient chain was to be
replaced by economic cooperation based on common interests.
Tolstoy still believed in the natural alliance of the two classes living
on the land, which would protect peasants from proletarianization
and landlords from ruin. Though he needed the income from the
land to sustain his growing family, money was not the main reason
Tolstoy chose to live in the country. He retreated to Yasnaya Polyana
to build a family utopia that would be a bastion against the advance
of modernity. Rural economy was only an auxiliary tool in this
campaign. His main battlefield was literature. By the end of 1862
he had closed down his village school and pedagogical magazine,
wondering why these occupations held his attention for so long.

Old debts still plagued him. Prior to his marriage he had lost a
considerable sum of money at the gambling table and had to borrow
1,000 roubles as an advance for *The Cossacks* from Mikhail Katkov,
the editor of the magazine *Russian Herald* (*Russkii vestnik*). At the
end of the 1850s many authors disillusioned with *Sovremennik* had
switched their allegiance to Katkov. A once moderate conservative
who was gradually turning into a morbid reactionary, Katkov was
no less successful and efficient as a publisher than Nekrasov. Katkov
provided an alternative to radical journalism and was supported
by the authorities. He gladly made the loan to Tolstoy and kept

rejecting all attempts by the repentant writer to repay the debt in money. Having settled in Yasnaya Polyana with a young wife, Tolstoy rushed to complete an overdue story.

The most difficult task facing him was to decide a natural outcome of Olenin's longing for Marianna. After numerous changes, Tolstoy came to a decision. Irritated by the constant womanizing of her suitor Lukashka, the bravest Cossack in the settlement, Marianna finally gives her consent to Olenin. After a quarrel with his bride, Lukashka loses his usual self-control and is mortally wounded by the Chechens. Full of remorse and hatred towards her unwanted admirer, Marianna throws Olenin out and he is left with no option but to go back to St Petersburg.

Katkov published *The Cossacks* immediately. The next issue of *Russian Herald* contained 'Polikushka', a short story mostly written abroad. The reading public welcomed the return of a favourite author. The critics admired *The Cossacks* and praised the vivid, nearly ethnographic portrayal of life in the settlement and the characters of Marianna, Lukashka and especially Yeroshka, the charismatic drunken old braggart and guardian of Cossack common law, lore and wisdom. Fet believed that *The Cossacks* was Tolstoy's best work so far. Turgenev was equally ecstatic, though much less appreciative of Olenin's spiritual quest. He recognized it as Tolstoy's self-portrait, but felt no personal sympathy for the author. Still, Turgenev was happy to greet the return of a wayward son of Russian literature and thankful for the card loss that had compelled Tolstoy to pick up his pen again.

The only person who was dissatisfied was Tolstoy himself, as he wrote in his diary in January 1863: 'Corrected the proofs of *The Cossacks* – it's terribly weak. Probably for that reason the public will be pleased with it' (*Ds*, p. 158). Though he had contemplated writing a sequel to the story if it were to be well received, Tolstoy never returned to *The Cossacks*, in spite of the public's nearly universal enthusiasm. By adding a subtitle – *A Caucasus Tale of 1852* – Tolstoy distanced himself from his narrative in time and placed it in the period preceding the Sebastopol stories. 'Who is this person who wrote *The Cossacks* and "Polikushka"? And what is the use of discussing them?' he wrote to Fet in early May 1863. '"Polikushka" is drivel on the first subject that comes into the head of a man who "wields a good pen", but *The Cossacks* has some pith in it, though it is bad' (*Ls*, I, p. 115). The 'pith' was Tolstoy's passionate attempt to dissolve himself in a wild and natural environment. Describing Olenin's fourteen-hour walks around the settlement, Tolstoy writes that no thought ever stirred in him during those strolls and he came home 'morally fresh, strong and completely happy' (*CW*, VI, p. 88).

In the same letter Tolstoy told Fet that he was working on the story of a horse known as 'The Strider'. Most of it is told in the first person of the horse. Criticism of social conventions from a 'natural' point of view had been popular since the eighteenth century, and horses, with their proximity to humans, could serve as ideal observers of their habits. Nevertheless, 'The Strider' was not a satirical allegory. Instead it conveyed Tolstoy's empathy with the plight of the animal and admiration for its calm acceptance of the order of life, decay and death. Tolstoy nearly completed the story, but did not publish it for more than twenty years until his wife rediscovered the manuscript in his papers. Work on 'The Strider' was halted when Tolstoy finally began writing his magnum opus.

Tolstoy drafted fifteen beginnings before he felt he could proceed. He was not yet sure of the plot, the names of the main characters, or the title of the book, but was certain that it was going to be a masterpiece. Never before, and arguably never after, was he so confident in himself. In October 1863 he wrote to Alexandra Tolstoy:

I've never felt my intellectual powers, and even all my moral powers, so free and so capable of work. And I have work to do. This work is a novel of the 1810s and 1820s, which has been occupying me fully since the autumn . . . Now, I am a writer with all the strength of my soul, and I write and I think as I have never thought or written before. (*Ls*, I, p. 118)

Preparing the first chapters for publication, Tolstoy informed Fet, with his usual self-denigration, that the new book, although he 'liked it more than his previous work, still seemed weak', but could not resist adding that what was to follow would be 'tremendous!!' (*Ls*, I, p. 193).

Historians define the decade that started with the abolition of serfdom in 1861 as the period of Great Reforms. In order to deal with tens of millions of newly acquired subjects, the emperor introduced limited local self-government, in the form of *zemstvos*, elected assemblies that were responsible for schools and health care. The government granted new independence to the judiciary and introduced trial by jury for criminal cases. University enrolments were greatly increased. A relative relaxation of censorship increased freedom of the press. Newspaper and magazine subscriptions soared and their pages soon filled with ardent and highly partisan discussions. Writers wrote novels about the issues, a popular shorthand for the most pressing problems of the day. Never in its history had Russia experienced a period of such public excitement. Tolstoy as ever went against the current. Isolated in Yasnaya Polyana, he was imagining a heroic past, when nobles and peasants were tied by a bond and could understand each other, and at the same time trying to recreate it in his own estate in an entirely different epoch and social environment.

By the mid-1860s a story about the amnesty of the rebellious aristocratic rebels had become obsolete. Tolstoy went back in time to explain the self-sacrifice of his heroes. *The Decembrists* started to morph into *War and Peace*. Common wisdom connected the birth of the Decembrist conspiracies with the glorious campaign that had taken the victorious Russian army to Paris in 1814. Young officers had liberated Europe and, in the process, had exposed themselves to European liberties. For Tolstoy, who stopped his narrative at the expulsion of French troops from Russia, the spirit of emancipation did not originate abroad, but emerged from the immediate contact between nobles and the Russian soldiery, mostly comprised of peasants in uniform.

Unlike Olenin in *The Cossacks*, Pierre Bezukhov did not have to suppress the demands of his intellect to draw closer to the peasant Platon Karataev. Their conversations in French captivity became a spiritual revelation for an inquisitive aristocrat. Likewise, Prince Andrei Bolkonsky experienced a feeling of unity with the soldiers he led into battle at Borodino. Mortally wounded, he was deprived of the chance to join the Decembrist conspirators of 1825, but in the epilogue, his fourteen-year-old son Nikolenka has a prophetic dream in which he participates in the rebellion. Nikolenka wakes up in tears, assured that his father would be proud of him.

According to Tolstoy, not all classes of Russian society took part in the birth of the nation. Courtiers and bureaucrats, unlike landowners, officers, peasants and soldiers, did not spend their lives on the land and in the fresh air. The notion of a nation as an organic body was foreign to them. Prince Andrei's initial infatuation with Mikhail Speransky, the mastermind of Alexander I's reforms, ended as he observed the great statesman's snow-white hands. The way of life and daily habits of a particular noble were far more important to Tolstoy than his political views. In the epilogue, Pierre joins the conspirators, while his brother-in-law Nikolai Rostov expresses his readiness to fight the rebels as his oath to the emperor commands him to do. Despite this, Nikolai and Pierre remain loving relatives, both deeply Russian in their convictions and loyalties.

In *Childhood* Tolstoy adopted the fictional worldview of a boy to create an idealized image of a noble estate. After the abolition of serfdom he gave an unashamedly nostalgic description of the serf economy. Nikolai is portrayed in the epilogue of *War and Peace* as a ruthless landowner, who abstains from beating his serfs only out of respect for the tender feelings of his wife. Still, 'long after his death the memory of his administration was devoutly preserved among the serfs', who remembered that he took care of them and put 'the peasant's affairs first and then his own' (*wp*, p. 1013).

In a draft of his introduction to the novel, Tolstoy confessed that he was afraid he would be 'guided by historical documents rather than by the truth' in his description of the events and 'important personages of 1812' (*wp*, p. 1087). He managed to overcome these doubts because of his conviction 'that nobody would ever tell what I had to tell'. He believed that 'specific qualities' of his 'development and personality' (*wp*, p. 1087) provided him with an access to historical knowledge better than any documents. This type of argumentation is typical of non-fiction, when an author explains the importance of his unique personal experience. Tolstoy used the same strategy in relation to the history of the Napoleonic wars. He searched for 'general laws' governing history, but believed that the way to discover these laws was to concentrate on 'artistic representation of the memories' (*cw*, xv, p. 132; xlviii, p. 87). In *Childhood*, the Sebastopol stories and *The Cossacks* he described events as directly witnessed by the narrator. Now he needed to introduce events that took place before he was born as if they were personal recollections.

To achieve this goal, Tolstoy inscribed the national epic into a family chronicle. The transparent play with surnames and the exact reproduction of real first names and patronymics of his ancestors, together with the meticulous description of the everyday lives of both families, provided the necessary aura of authenticity. To be sure, the disenchanted aristocratic liberal Nikolai Tolstoy had little to do with the brave officer and passionate rural landowner Nikolai Rostov. Likewise, the educated and enlightened Maria Volkonsky did not resemble pious and humble Maria Bolkonsky. Tolstoy sought rather to achieve a general impression of the historical reconstruction of a family history, not to render all the details in the most accurate way.

The story of Nikolai and Maria, however, is only an auxiliary plot in the novel. Tolstoy used a more sophisticated approach in dealing with the main characters. He divided his authorial alter ego between Pierre Bezukhov, in whom dissipated habits, emotional and intellectual instability and lust competed with innate kindness, an ardent desire for moral goodness and admiration for the simple wisdom of the Russian peasant, and Prince Andrei with his quest for glory, Napoleonic ambitions and aristocratic arrogance. Each character had to resolve one of the two existential problems that tormented Tolstoy throughout his life: the power of sexuality and the fear of death. Pierre was to show the author and the reader how to handle erotic passions, Andrei how to deal with mortality.

In *War and Peace* these intractable existential problems are happily resolved. Pierre manages to tame his instincts in marriage. Prince Andrei, having nearly recovered from his mortal wound, chooses eternal universal life over personal existence and celestial over earthly human love. In Tolstoy's early works, only simple and unreflective people were blessed with graceful exits. This time he awarded a radiant death to the character representing the lofty part of his soul, while the earthly part stayed alive to enjoy carnal pleasures in a way that is morally irreproachable. In the first version of the novel, which Tolstoy provisionally entitled *All Is Well that Ends Well*, Prince Andrei voluntarily cedes Natasha to his friend. In the final text, all ends even better: Tolstoy suggests that Pierre's eventual success in the struggle between the author's competing alter egos for the heart of the same woman is more than just a consequence of

Prince Andrei's death. It is a reassuring victory of the real over the ethereal, of this world over the next.

In the 1860s Tolstoy was not yet the avowed pacifist he later became. He abhorred the senseless loss of human life, but still regarded a fight against invaders as the natural and therefore legitimate instinct of a people protecting their own land. Reconciling his image of the war with his anarchist credo was difficult. Even the most consistent opponents of the state grudgingly agree that war is the prerogative of central authority. Tolstoy was never ready to compromise his beliefs or make partial concessions. He developed a provocative and controversial theory of historical process defined not 'by power . . . but by the activity of all the people who participate in the events' (*wp*, p. 1061). Rulers, leaders or military commanders only pretend to govern millions of individuals, but in fact succumb to the cumulative force of their wills.

At Yasnaya Polyana Tolstoy favoured beekeeping over other agricultural activities. He spent hours and days observing bees in their hives and comparing their seemingly chaotic, but perfectly choreographed, flights with the movement of human masses. In 1864 he sent Katkov a translation of Karl Vogt's article on bees, which had been completed at his instigation by Elizaveta Bers, writing in the accompanying letter: 'I've become an ardent beekeeper, and so I can judge' (*Ls*, I, p. 185). Katkov never published the article. He expected a novel from his famous author, not an agricultural treatise. The progress of the novel was, however, slow and difficult. Rebuilding the hive of history was impossible without tracing the trajectories of individual bees. Tolstoy believed that 'a month in the life of a single sixteenth-century peasant' (*cw*, XVI, p. 126) was as legitimate a topic for historical research as was the history of the whole of Europe. His iconoclastic philosophy of history demanded equally unconventional psychology.

Tolstoy began by challenging the concept of 'the person' that traditionally constituted a foundation of literature and moral philosophy. In preparatory notebooks to his novel he claimed to have discovered the new law of 'subordination of personality to its movement in time', which 'demands that we reject the inner conscience of the unmovable unity of our personality' (*cw*, xv, pp. 233–4). Thoughts, feelings and decisions of a given individual have very little to do with his or her conscious preferences, but are the result of numerous impulses that keep any individual soul in constant flux.

When Pierre first sees Natasha after the war, he fails initially to recognize the woman he had loved all his life and from whom he had been separated for only a few short months. Her sufferings had made her an entirely different person. When Natasha smiles, however, her image in Pierre's eyes is restored and his enduring love and longing revive. This episode is breathtakingly convincing and powerful precisely because of its psychological improbability. In the ensuing conversation Pierre tells Natasha how 'shocked' he was by the news of his wife's death and how 'very sorry' for her he felt (*wp*, p. 987). However, a month and a dozen pages earlier he is described by Tolstoy as 'remembering . . . that his wife is no more' and repeating to himself 'Oh how good! How splendid!' (*wp*, p. 976). Pierre is not trying to deceive his beloved. He has forgotten his recent feelings and thoughts so completely because Natasha's attentive gaze made him an entirely different person and parts of his previous experience have ceased to exist.

Tolstoy considered the failed elopement of Natasha with Anatole Kuragin 'the most difficult part and the keypoint of the whole novel' (*Ls*, p. 143). Natasha was ready to succumb to Kuragin's seduction not because she had ceased loving Prince Andrei. On the contrary, on the eve of his imminent return her expectation had reached its highest pitch, making her especially sensitive to erotic infatuation. Yet, on a deeper level, her fatal decision reveals a hidden fear of the pending marriage. Love for her fiancé notwithstanding, her sexual instincts draw her to Pierre, as she somehow senses that he is the man with whom she could have numerous healthy children. In the initial version of *War and Peace*, finished in 1866, the mutual unconscious attraction of Pierre and Natasha is much more explicit. At the end, Prince Andrei, exasperated by his bride's incomprehensible betrayal, asks Sonya whether 'Natasha has ever loved anyone deeply?' 'There is one, it's Bezukhov,' said Sonya. 'But she does not even know it herself.'[2]

The story Sonya Bers wrote and gave to Lev before their marriage was entitled 'Natasha'. It dealt with an intense rivalry between two elder sisters, but the main character was their naive and charming youngest sibling. Tanya Bers had herself chosen the name for her literary representation and Tolstoy followed her example. In a letter to Mikhail Bashilov, the first illustrator of the novel, he asked the artist to 'model Natasha on Tanichka [diminutive of Tanya] Bers'. He was sure that, 'having seen a daguerreotype of Tanya when she was 12, then her picture in white blouse when she was 16, and then her big portrait last year', Bashilov 'won't fail to make use of this model and its stages of development which are so close to my model' (*Ls*, I, p. 209).

Tanya (Tatiana) Bers was not beautiful, as her portraits testify. According to Ilya Tolstoy, Lev's second son, 'her mouth was too large, she had a slightly receding chin, and she was just the least bit squint-eyed, but all this only accentuated her extraordinary femininity and allure.'[3] All Tolstoy's children, who remembered her as a middle-aged married woman marked by deep personal drama and loss, spoke about the fire burning in her and the joy of life that captivated and infected those around her with a sense of happiness. When Tolstoy and Sofia married, Tanya was sixteen. She quickly established a personal bond with her future brother-in-law. She was on first-name terms with him before her elder sisters and then began to call him by the even more familiar diminutive Levochka.

Like many people endowed with a choleric temperament, Tolstoy was prone to wild hilarity. His youngest daughter,

Tatiana Bers in 1862.

Alexandra, born when he was 56, remembered him laughing 'unrestrainedly like a very young creature, interrupting his laughter with groans of exhaustion, swinging his body, blowing his nose and wiping away his tears' (*AT*, I, p. 238). His laughter was also highly infectious. Tanya Bers, brimming with vitality, became for him a companion of choice. She was a frequent guest at Yasnaya Polyana and spent hours with him at his hives and on fishing and hunting trips. Shortly after the marriage, Sofia recorded in the diary 'unpleasant feelings towards Tanya', who she believed was 'pushing herself too close in Levochka's life' (SAT-DS, p. 73). The young countess was unconsciously replicating the reaction of her elder sister to her own romance with Tolstoy several months earlier.

Tanya was an accomplished singer and Lev enjoyed accompanying her on the piano. As Alexandra writes, her 'singing and voice had the same elusive charm, harmony and contained passion as all her character' (AT, I, p. 269). Tolstoy was receptive to this 'contained passion'. 'Tanya – sensuality', he remarked in his diary three months after his marriage. Two weeks later he added: 'Tanya – the charm of naiveté; egoism and intuition' (Ds, pp. 151, 157). His letters to her are full of funny nonsense worthy of *Alice's Adventures in Wonderland* and of paternal advice 'to guard her heart' as 'the mark on the tormented heart remains forever':

> Remember Katerina Yegorovna's words: never add sour cream to a fancy pastry. I know that the artistic demands of your rich nature are not the same as the demands of ordinary girls of your age; but Tanya, as an experienced man, who loves you not just because we are relations, I am telling you the whole truth. Tanya, remember Mme Laborde; her legs are too fat for her body – a fact which you can easily observe with a little care when she comes on to the stage in pantaloons. (Ls, I, pp. 113–14)

'I took Tanya, added Sonya, stirred it up and got Natasha' (AT, I, p. 270), once said Tolstoy listing the ingredients of his most charming female character, who infuses *War and Peace* with an atmosphere of love and fullness of being. Sofia's presence is evident only in the epilogue, when Natasha unexpectedly turns into a devoted, commanding, jealous wife and caring mother. In the body of the novel Tanya seems to have been the author's only source of inspiration. However, the transformation Tolstoy imagined for Natasha never occurred to her main prototype in real life. Long after her marriage Tanya Bers retained her irrepressible, exuberant femininity.

At the time of Tolstoy's short but passionate courtship of her elder sister, Tanya was enjoying a teenage romance with her cousin Alexander Kuzminsky. The description of Natasha's first kiss with Boris Drubetskoy at the beginning of the novel was based on a confession made by Tanya to Tolstoy. Tanya's subsequent amorous adventures gave Tolstoy new material for the development of his plot as he was writing. In St Petersburg in 1863 she had a brief but intense infatuation with Anatole Shostak, who had a reputation as a notorious seducer. Anatole followed Tanya to Yasnaya Polyana, where they had a scandalous rendezvous in the forest, after which Sofia and Leo drove him out of the house. In her memoirs Tanya wrote that the next time she saw Anatole was twenty years later. Yet Sofia's letters to Leo reveal that Anatole returned to the estate when Tolstoy was absent and that his flirtation with Tanya continued even during the early stages of her next romance, one that was to have far more dramatic consequences.

Tolstoy's only remaining elder brother, Sergei, was living near Yasnaya Polyana. He lacked Leo's literary talent and spiritual curiosity, but had a similarly wild temperament. Unlike Leo, he was handsome. For nearly fifteen years he had been living openly with a Gypsy singer, Masha Shishkina, and they had several children. When Leo introduced him to the Berses, Sergei could not hide his astonishment that his brother had chosen Sonya over Tanya. He fell in love with Tanya and managed to conquer her heart, a process that was perhaps helped by her mimetic desire to join the Tolstoy family. Sergei, however, remained hesitant and torn between his new passion and his existing family. He pleaded with Tanya not to reject him, fixed deadlines for a final choice

Sergei Tolstoy and Tatiana Bers at the time of their romance.

and kept postponing them, promised to visit her for a decisive rendezvous and never appeared. Driven into a state of utter despair, Tanya tried to poison herself, but fortunately changed her mind and was saved.

The catastrophe seemed to have broken these tortured relations, but in June 1865, having met Tanya in Yasnaya Polyana, Sergei once again fell under her charms and proposed, which was accepted. Marriages between in-laws were forbidden by the Orthodox Church, so the couple planned a secret wedding that could later be legalized with the help of Leo's connections at court. These plans collapsed in less than two weeks. In spite of his proposal, Sergei was still not sure whom he should marry. He claimed that having seen Masha's solitary prayer, he felt unable to leave his old partner, but also complained that Masha's parents had blackmailed him by threatening to denounce his proposed marriage to Tanya as illegal. Both versions could have been true. Indignant and humiliated, Tanya released Sergei from his vows. Finally, she became repentant about the whole affair and ashamed of her role in it. More than a year after this, her health remained precarious.

Unable to return to Yasnaya Polyana, Tanya went to recover at the estate of Dmitry Dyakov, a man who had been a model of *comme il faut* behaviour and an object of homoerotic veneration for Tolstoy in his younger days. Dyakov also fell under the spell of Tanya's charm. Once, in response to her desperate self-blame, he told her that, were he free, he would have immediately proposed to her. Dyakov's wife died shortly afterwards, and he did as he had promised. Tolstoy strongly advised his sister-in-law to accept, probably hoping to keep her within his close circle of friends and relatives or in an attempt to bring actual life closer to the plot he devised, but Tanya chose Kuzminsky, who was still waiting for his chance. They married in August 1867. According to family legend, on their way to the church they encountered Sergei and Masha, also heading to their wedding.

A year earlier Tanya had sung before Fet and his wife at the Dyakovs'. Fet knew her story, knew that doctors had advised her against singing, as it was considered damaging to her lungs, and probably had in mind the suspected suicide of his own former love, Maria Lazich, also an excellent singer. Eleven years later, having again listened to Tatiana's singing in Yasnaya Polyana, he recalled her earlier impressions in one of the most beautiful love poems in the Russian language:

> You sang until the dawn, worn out to the point of tears, Now love means you, and you alone, no other love but you, And I then longed to live, my love, that all my living years, I could love you and embrace you and shed my tears for you.[4]

Tolstoy appreciated the poem, but not the feeling behind it, 'Why does he want to embrace our Tanya, he is a married man?' (*Kuz*, pp. 400–401), he asked, characteristically failing to discriminate between life and art.

Tolstoy ignored Tanya's plea not to make her intimate life public. He needed the details he had witnessed as well as those she had confessed to him to achieve the verisimilitude he desired. He did not even bother to rename her first admirer. Tanya's love, impatience, despair and repentance served as a model for the story of Natasha's relations with Anatole Kuragin and Pierre's reaction to her shame and sorrow. When, on the eve of publication in 1868, Kuzminsky found out that the illustrator had modelled the image of Natasha on his wife, he ordered his family to leave Moscow. He also wanted to sever ties with the Tolstoys, but Tanya refused, declaring that she owed 'everything good and holy in herself to Levochka' (*Kuz*, p. 444). She knew Tolstoy had created her as a person and her brilliantly written and perceptive, if not entirely reliable, memoirs show to what extent she had internalized the image of Natasha Rostova. Unfortunately the memoirs stop around the time of her marriage, though the Kuzminskys continued visiting Yasnaya Polyana for many years.

In his memoirs Tolstoy's son Ilya confessed that he had often asked himself, 'whether papa was in love with Aunt Tanya', and finally became convinced that he was. Ilya rushes to explain that there was nothing impure in this love resembling a sort of '*amitié amoureuse*',[5] of which Tolstoy himself could have been unaware. Tolstoy's wife, full of deep resentment towards her great husband, wrote in her late memoirs that his relations with his sister-in-law could have ended badly had it not been for her romance with Sergei. This is highly unlikely. For both Tolstoy and Tanya any sort of affair would have been more than unthinkable. At the same time Tolstoy, with his lifelong habit of introspection, could hardly be unaware of his feelings. *War and Peace* is arguably the longest and the most exquisite declaration of love ever written by any man to any woman. Tanya was present at the first reading of the opening chapters and wrote about her impressions in a letter to Polivanov, Sofia's rejected suitor. Those listening, she told Polivanov, liked Pierre 'less than all the others', but she liked him 'more than all the others', because she 'loved people like that' (*Kuz*, p. 319). Clearly Tanya had understood the point.

The first two instalments of the novel appeared in the January and February 1865 issues of the *Russian Herald* under the title '1805'. It was clear to all that this title was bound to change and that the narrative would develop beyond that year. Tolstoy's focus was not a set period, defined in the title, but the flow of time. These two instalments were followed a year later by three more, printed in the same issue as the first chapter of Dostoevsky's *Crime and Punishment*. However, while Dostoevsky kept to the discipline and provided successive chapters until the end of the year, Tolstoy's readers had to wait longer. Responding to readers' interest, Tolstoy decided to switch from serial publication in a periodical to separate volumes: '1805' was therefore republished in book form at the end of 1866. The first full draft of the novel was finished by the end of 1866, but then Tolstoy began revising or rather rewriting the text. It took another two years before four reworked volumes appeared in 1868, this time entitled *War and Peace*. The two final volumes completed the publication in 1869.

The narrative in *War and Peace* concludes in an open-ended way. In the epilogue, Pierre returns from St Petersburg, where he helps to launch a conspiratorial society, to enjoy marital bliss. The ordeals of the family seem to be over, yet every reader knew what awaited the characters in the near future. Months of captivity in the retreating French army, the Great Fire of Moscow and Count Rostov's carriages full of wounded officers would pale into insignificance compared with the thirty years that Pierre would have to spend doing hard labour and as an exile in Siberia as a punishment for the Decembrist revolt in 1825, with Natasha sharing her husband's hardships. History may have reached a lull that coincides with the last page of the novel, but it will return with a vengeance soon enough.

When preparing the first chapters for the *Russian Herald*, Tolstoy begged Fet for his thoughts: 'I value your opinion, and that of a man whom I dislike all the more the older I get – Turgenev.

He will understand' (*Ls*, i, p. 193). Fet sent Tolstoy several letters full of glowing praise, complemented later by a poem in which he wrote that he 'stood in holy awe before the elemental force' of Tolstoy's genius.[6] Contrary to Tolstoy's expectations, Turgenev at first failed to understand. He found '1805' 'positively bad, boring and unsuccessful', and was especially irritated by Tolstoy's 'petty psychological observations'. He could not believe that the author 'places this unfortunate product higher than *The Cossacks*!' With the publication of new volumes, Turgenev gradually changed his opinion, but still could not forgive Tolstoy his 'philosophizing' and 'Slavophilism' (*WP*, pp. 1107–8).

Critical reaction was mixed: the book did not fit into any literary category that existed at the time. Tolstoy himself insisted that his book 'is not a novel, even less is it a poem, and still less a historical chronicle' (*WP*, p. 1090) and expected the reviewers to guide the reader through the complex threads, and not to juxtapose his art with his philosophy. In his diary he likened the critics, who admired 'the sleigh ride at Christmas, Bagration's attack, the hunt, the dinner, the dancing', but not 'the theory of history and philosophy', to dogs who believe that the ingredients thrown out by a cook are the actual meal he is preparing (*Ds*, p. 170). He wished to be acknowledged as the first and the best. When his brother-in-law, a military officer, asked him why he was so nervous about the opinion of the critics, Tolstoy replied: 'You want to be a general, I also want to be a literary general' (*Kuz*, p. 333).

Tolstoy got the promotion he craved. The public was impatient to read the new literary sensation. No book in the history of Russian literature had ever been received with such enthusiasm and none earned its author such profits as *War and Peace*. It largely exceeded the revenues generated by Tolstoy's estate. Critics also gradually began to recognize the novel's greatness. Nikolai Strakhov, a Slavophile thinker who was to become a close friend of Tolstoy, wrote in the January 1870 issue of the magazine *Zarya* (Dawn):

The picture of human life is complete. The picture of the Russian of those days is complete. The picture of what we call history and the struggle of nations is complete. The picture of everything that people consider to be their happiness and greatness, their sorrow and their humiliation is complete. That is what *War and Peace* is. (*WP*, p. 1102)

The marriage and the novel put an end to Tolstoy's gambling. The stakes from both endeavours could hardly be any higher. While the result of Tolstoy's bet on family life was at best uncertain, his gamble on *War and Peace* had definitely broken the bank.

Victory is a mixed blessing, for there is always the day after. For Tolstoy the reckoning began even before he had finished proofreading the last volume of *War and Peace*. In August 1869 he travelled to Penza Province to buy an estate. The price of land was rising; Tolstoy finally had spare cash that he planned to invest. Staying in a coaching inn in the small town of Arzamas, he suddenly fell into a prolonged state of unbearable panic and felt himself close to death. Tolstoy wrote about it to his wife and fifteen years later, at an entirely different period of his life, described it in an unfinished story 'Notes of a Madman', named after the eponymous tale by Gogol:

Why have I come here? Where am I taking myself? Why and where am I escaping? I am running away from something dreadful and cannot escape it. I am always with myself and it is I who am my own tormentor. Here I am, the whole of me. Neither Penza nor any other property will add anything to or take anything from me. It is myself I am weary of and find intolerable and such a torment . . . 'What foolishness this is!' I asked myself, 'why am I depressed, what am I afraid of?' 'Me', answered the voice of Death, inaudibly, 'I am here!' A cold shudder ran down my back. Yes! Death! It will come – here it is – and it is not ought to be. Had I actually been facing death, I could not have suffered as much as I did then. Then I should have been frightened. But I was not frightened now. I saw and felt the approach of death is advancing and at the same time I felt that such a thing ought not to exist. My whole soul was conscious of the necessity and right to live, and yet I felt that Death was being accomplished . . . There is nothing to life. Death is the only real thing, and death ought not to be . . . Something was tearing my soul apart and could not complete the action. (*TSF*, pp. 307–8)

As ever, Tolstoy's analysis is mercilessly detailed and precise. He is not writing about the fear of death – the narrator knows he is not dying. The object of his horror is the sudden physical awareness of one's own mortality, the omnipresence of death that makes life senseless. The scale of despair was proportionate to the intensity of his attachment to life, the inner conviction of 'a necessity and a right to live'. Death, Tolstoy was sure, 'ought not to be', yet at the same time, it was a reality and the only reality.

Such feelings were not new to him. Tolstoy was always prone to bouts of anxiety and depression and this time he was terribly overworked and exhausted. The 'Arzamas horror' caught him when he was completing the book in which he intended to give a convincing solution of an enigma of death. Still, that liberating feeling of universal love, with which Prince Andrei left the world, eluded him. There was no way of forgetting or reconciling oneself to death.

A day before leaving for Penza, Tolstoy wrote to Fet telling him that he had spent the entire summer reading German philosophy. He had always believed that abstract reasoning had no value unless connected to actual moral issues, but now, approaching the end of his monumental work, he searched for a general justification for human existence. Tolstoy found Hegel an 'empty collection of phrases', appreciated Kant, but Schopenhauer gave him 'spiritual

Tolstoy at forty years old, in 1868, after he had just finished *War and Peace*.

joy' he 'had never experienced before'. Tolstoy told Fet, an old admirer of the German philosopher, that he found Schopenhauer 'the most brilliant of men' (*Ls*, 1, p. 221) and offered to produce a joint translation of his works, the job that later Fet had to accomplish alone.

Schopenhauer believed that the driving force for all our decisions, passions and ambitions is an unconscious 'will to live'. The desires provoked by the will to live are 'unlimited, their claims inexhaustible, and every satisfied desire gives birth to a new one'. The human mind is able only to produce illusionary goals hiding from an individual bound for destruction, the futility imminent in all his wishes and labours. In reality, 'nothing whatever is worth our exertions, our efforts and our struggles, all good things are empty and fleeting, the world on all sides is bankrupt, and life is a business which does not cover the costs.'[7]

This vision was close to Tolstoy's cherished notion of the human beehive, in which the movement of bees is driven by a natural force beyond individual control. Although the idea of a will to live comes across in *War and Peace* as a fundamentally benign force, the influence of the great German pessimist is evident in the second epilogue of the novel. As he approached the end of his magnum opus, Tolstoy was gradually losing his optimism. Schopenhauer had helped him to reassess his views.

In 1865 Petr Boborykin, the editor of the magazine *Reader's Library* and one of the most prolific writers of his time, asked Tolstoy for a contribution. Boborykin was a highly popular author but is now remembered mostly because of the reply Tolstoy drafted but decided not to send:

Problems of the local self-government, literature and emancipation of women etc. . . . are not only not interesting in the world of art; they have no place there at all . . . The aims of art are incommensurable (as the mathematicians say) with social aims. The aim of the artist is not to solve a problem irrefutably, but to make people love life in all its countless inexhaustible manifestations. If I were to be told that I could write a novel whereby I might irrefutably establish what seemed to me the correct point of view on all social problems, I would not even devote two hours' work to such a novel; but if I were to be told that what I should write would be read in about 20 years' time by those who are now children, and that they would laugh and cry over it and love life, I would devote all my life and all my energies to it. (*Ls*, I, p. 197)

Tolstoy wanted his novel to bring him money and fame, but these petty goals were secondary to his desire to tackle the most pressing existential problems. What compelled him to spend seven years chained to his desk was his hope of making people fall in love with life. His own drama, however, was that having completed his task he found himself unable to love life himself; moreover, he desperately hated it. He wrote to Fet in January 1871: 'I've stopped writing and will never again write verbose nonsense like *War and Peace*. I am guilty, but I swear I'll never do it again' (*Ls*, I, p. 230).

In 1884, when going over the history of his discord with his wife in his diary, Tolstoy remembered the early 1870s as the time 'when the string snapped' and he 'became aware of his loneliness' (*Ds*, p. 188). Never before were his depressions so acute. Sofia, who had already witnessed a lot, was appalled to see her hyperactive husband lying motionless on the sofa, staring at the ceiling and pleading with her to leave him alone and let him die peacefully. He was afraid he would go insane and felt that everything was finished for him.

In the 1850s, during his previous, much less powerful crisis, Tolstoy had turned to teaching, which helped to lift the depression. Now he decided to try the same path and resumed the old challenge. In January 1872 a new school for peasants opened in the house at Yasnaya Polyana, with Sofia and their elder children Sergei and Tatiana helping Tolstoy. The circumstances, however, were very different this time. The introduction of local self-government had yielded remarkably quick results. Popular education was no longer uncharted territory. Village schools had proliferated; hundreds of future teachers were studying new methods in universities and seminaries. Twelve years earlier Tolstoy had tried to popularize his approaches to teaching through an educational magazine. This time he decided that speaking to teachers was useless and that he needed to address pupils themselves. He started compiling the *ABC* (*Azbuka*) and *Russian Books for Reading* (*The Primer*), which he began to publish the same year with the help of Sofia and Strakhov, who had become an ardent convert to Tolstoy's way of thinking and an eager assistant in all his enterprises.

The *ABC* and *Russian Books for Reading* came out between 1872 and 1875, and again in 1878–9 in different versions. Tolstoy could never republish his work without editing and sometimes completely rewriting it. For the first time in his life he was writing not about, but for 'the people'. He planned to give lessons in basic reading, arithmetic, natural sciences and morality to millions. His preparations were, as usual, extensive; he perused collections of Russian folk songs, fables and proverbs, the Lives of the Saints that constituted the main source of religious instruction for the majority of peasants, books on mathematics, physics, astronomy and pedagogical literature written by British and American authors involved in organizing summer schools for working-class children.

It was also a painstaking literary experiment; the stylistic idiom he had elaborated over many years of effort was thrown into the dustbin as 'verbose nonsense'. No longer could he afford rich vocabulary, complicated syntax, expressive details, powerful metaphors, digressions or meticulous psychological analysis. The texts he included in his books vary in length from two or three sentences to several pages and are uniformly plain, dry and simple.

Works of art usually lend themselves to different interpretations, but the ABC and *The Primer* leave no room for ambiguity: the moral lesson needed to be evident to all and without any explanation:

> The poor man came to the rich man to beg. The rich man did not give him anything and said: 'Go away'. The poor man did not leave, then the rich man became angry and threw a stone at him. The poor man took the stone, put it close to his bosom and said: 'I'll keep this stone until I can throw it at him'. It happened this way. The rich man did a bad thing; they took everything from him and led him to prison. When he went to prison, the poor man came, wanting to throw the stone at him, and then he thought again and dropped the stone on the ground, saying: For nothing, did I carry this stone: when he was rich and strong, I was afraid of him and now I pity him. (CW, XXII, pp. 84–5)

The story illustrates the Russian saying 'to keep a stone in one's bosom', which means 'to bear a grudge'. Tolstoy tells the story about the uselessness of revenge and the advantages of forgiveness without abstract words and moral notions, to make it accessible to a six-year-old who has just learned to read. In the same way, when introducing elementary natural sciences he avoided talking about laws, concentrating instead on observable phenomena like the yearly cycle of the seasons, the effects of heat and cold, rain and the evaporation of water. He also invented his own technique for teaching the alphabet that was, from his point of view, better suited to a child who could not attend school regularly.

The first reaction among professional teachers was negative. Tolstoy failed to receive the approval from the Ministry of Education that was required for school textbooks. Reviews were nearly unanimously hostile. His financial loss amounted to 2,000 roubles, not a critical sum of money, but nonetheless substantial. In his response to the critics, Tolstoy wrote that he was so 'sure that his books meet the basic needs of the Russian people' that he did not even bother to give explanations; as a baker, giving bread to the hungry, does not explain how they should consume it (*CW*, XXI, p. 409)

Tolstoy was suggesting a free schooling system with diverse curricula and teaching methods, based on peasants' immediate needs and the kind of education they wanted to give to their children. He would never agree that academics, educators, government bureaucrats or elected representatives had a right to decide how or what to teach to peasants. His opponents believed in a standardized national educational system that Russia was still lacking. They wanted to prepare pupils for the new life that their parents could not possibly envisage. Tolstoy aspired to give them the necessary tools to improve their traditional way of life without changing it.

Once again, Tolstoy was engaged in an uphill struggle and continued fighting against the odds. In 1874–5 he completely rewrote his book and produced the *New ABC*, which was finally granted approval for use in schools. Sales soared. In Tolstoy's lifetime the *New ABC* and *Russian Books for Reading* went through 28 editions, selling 2 million copies. They were not accepted as manuals and textbooks, but were considered an essential part of early reading. At the very least, this was a good starting point for the continuation of the crusade, but by the mid-1870s Tolstoy's interests were already far from the classroom.

During his personal crisis in the late 1850s and early '60s Tolstoy had stopped publishing, but continued writing and searching for a new path forward. Now he did the same thing. For a while he contemplated turning from prose to drama. In February 1870 he wrote to Fet that 'all this winter' he had been 'occupied solely with drama' and that 'characters in a tragedy and comedy begin to act' (*Ls*, I, p. 225). He had already authored two rather mediocre comedies directed against nihilism and the emancipation of women. Many years later he would return to writing for the stage with considerable success. This time, however, his dramatic designs remained unrealized. Unlike many nineteenth-century realists, in his novels Tolstoy did not withdraw from the text in order to create an illusion of objectivity. Instead he pushed himself to the front, ceaselessly commenting, moralizing and guiding the reader. A play form did not allow for such authorial projections. Compelled to hide himself behind his characters, he lost confidence.

One of his plans concerned the period of Peter the Great and his Westernizing reforms that engendered a Europeanized elite in a profoundly non-European country. In *War and Peace* Tolstoy had looked for the ways to remedy this rupture; now he wanted to go back to its roots. Having established a subject, Tolstoy decided to shift the form from drama to historical novel, a genre much more comfortable to him.

Historians always emphasized the personal role of the tsar in the Westernization of Russia, but this approach contradicted Tolstoy's philosophy of history. For the start of the novel, he chose the confrontation between the young tsar and his sister Sophia, then acting as a regent. Peter escaped from Moscow to the Troitsky (Trinity) monastery, leaving his sister in the Kremlin and thus allowing people to switch loyalties, moving from one camp to another. Tolstoy compared this precarious moment to a tilt in the scales: when someone starts pouring grain on one side, the opposite side with the weight stays, at first, solidly in place, but an extra handful suddenly lifts it in the air, where it hangs in the balance and any light touch may tip it either way.

Tolstoy's research for the new novel was even more intensive and profound than when he had written about 1812. He studied chronicles, copied out words and expressions from historical dictionaries, read books about everyday life in the period. In spite of all this he struggled to empathize with his characters – they were too remote. He could not achieve the desired effect of immediate presence, when the actions and words of the protagonists give the impression of having been recorded from reality rather than invented. His wife was right when she wrote to her sister that 'all the characters of the time of Peter the Great are ready, dressed and put in their places, but do not breathe' (*cw*, XVII, p. 632). She expressed the hope that they might yet come to life.

This was, of course, far from impossible. Tolstoy knew how to rework his drafts and cope with narrative problems. He believed that 'the whole knot of Russian life resides' in the Petrine period and wanted to unravel it. But the deeper Tolstoy delved into the end of the seventeenth century, the more clearly he saw that he would be unable to proceed. In December 1872 he wrote to Strakhov that 'he has surrounded himself with books about Peter I and his time, made efforts to write, but could not' (*cw*, XVII, pp. 629–30). Suddenly he found himself writing a novel in which the action was proceeding in the immediate present.

In March 1873 Tolstoy finally started writing the new novel in earnest. This time his progress was quick: in May he informed Strakhov that he had finished a novel 'in draft form' (*AK*, p. 747) and in September wrote to him that he would be completing the novel soon. This was somewhat premature, but in the second half of 1874 Tolstoy started thinking about publication. In November Tolstoy asked Katkov to pay him the hefty sum of 10,000 roubles as an advance payment. When Katkov started bargaining, Tolstoy approached Nekrasov, who had acquired the magazine *Notes of Fatherland* after *Sovremennik* had been closed by the authorities. When Nekrasov expressed interest, Katkov doubled the advance. On 1 January 1875, Strakhov congratulated Tolstoy on having been paid 20,000 roubles, 'an unheard price for a novel'.[8]

The first instalments of *Anna Karenina* appeared in the *Russian Herald* from January to April 1875, then from January to April 1876 and from December 1876 to April 1877. The long intervals were caused by Tolstoy's characteristic procrastination, and his slow and painstaking rewriting and editing of the text. At the same time, this peculiar rhythm of publication helped the illusion that the plot was unfolding in real time. The novel, as it progressed, absorbed events taking place in the outside world: the consequences of military reform, fresh court intrigues, a visit by a foreign opera company to St Petersburg and the country sliding into war with the Ottoman Empire. Katkov's publications were the main force rallying public opinion around the Slavic cause: the national movements in Bulgaria and Serbia fighting against the Turks for independence. In April 1877 an initially reluctant emperor bowed to public pressure and declared war. Political developments that could not have been envisaged when Tolstoy started his novel filled its pages and changed the fates of the characters.

Tolstoy was wary of the Panslavicist and imperialist ideology espoused by the *Russian Herald*. In the last part of the book he resoundingly attacked the war and the bellicose spirit of its proponents. The final chapters were prepared for publication in the May 1877 issue, but Katkov insisted on cutting the most explicit passages. When Tolstoy rejected this demand, Katkov refused to publish the ending, instead providing readers with a very short summary and a reference to a full edition under preparation. Infuriated, Tolstoy answered with an indignant letter and cut all relations with the editor. The last part appeared as a separate publication in June 1877, and the full text, once again revised with Strakhov's help, in January 1878.

Notwithstanding this scandal, the ideological orientation of *Anna Karenina* made it more appropriate for a conservative magazine than a progressive one. Tolstoy was writing a novel about adultery. The problem of the emancipation of women was not confined to post-reform Russia, it was one of the most prevalent issues in European thought and social practice at that time. Despite the remarks he had made in an unsent letter to Boborykin, this problem had always deeply concerned Tolstoy. In 1863, when he began working on *War and Peace*, his old foe Chernyshevsky had smuggled out a revolutionary novel from captivity in the Peter and Paul Fortress in St Petersburg. The incredible incompetence of the Russian censors had allowed Nekrasov to publish *What Is to Be Done?* in *Sovremennik*. Artistically weak, it made an easy target for the critics, but it was the first book in Russia to deal with the problem of sexual compatibility and to suggest divorce and cohabitation as possible solutions to family problems. Tolstoy had already refuted Chernyshevsky in the epilogue to *War and Peace*, but his rage was still boiling.

In 1868 Tolstoy drafted an imagined conversation with his female would-be critics, in which he argued that the highest and most sacred mission of a woman was motherhood. No great man, argued Tolstoy, who lost his mother at the age of two, had ever been brought up without maternal care. In the following year John Stuart Mill published his essay *The Subjection of Women*, forcefully arguing for gender equality. The essay achieved immediate fame and was twice translated into Russian. In a polemical reply, Strakhov reiterated the idea of the sanctity of familial bonds, but conceded that 'sexless' women, who had failed to discover their true calling or passed their procreative age, could possibly benefit from formal education and social activity.

Such compromises were not in Tolstoy's nature: he wrote a letter to Strakhov, fully supporting his main argument but insisting that there are no 'sexless' women, 'just as there are no four-legged people' (*Ls*, 1, p. 227). Those not fortunate enough to have their own families could help bring up other women's children. Tolstoy went so far as to repeat Schopenhauer's assertion that prostitutes helping to channel away the excesses of male sexuality are more socially beneficial than the women working in offices. Probably unwilling to scandalize his correspondent, whom he had not yet met personally, Tolstoy decided against sending the letter.

For an old bachelor like Strakhov, the questions raised by Mill were an intellectual problem; for Tolstoy they were of existential importance. He had married believing that marriage could redeem sexuality. After seven years of family life, he concluded that sexuality itself undermined and corrupted marriage. In 1872, in a letter to his spinster aunt Alexandra Tolstoy, Lev compared the forthcoming wedding of his favourite niece Varvara to a 'sacrifice, an immolation on the altar of some terrible and cynical deity' (*Ls*, I, p. 241). No doubt he was thinking about the eighteen-year-old virgin 'sacrificed' in the carriage after his wedding. He blamed his premarital past, when he had irreversibly debauched himself and could not help debauching his wife by awakening her sexual desires. Shortly before the marriage of Tanya and Kuzminsky, Tolstoy told Sofia that he was afraid of and disliked the sensuality he noticed in the couple. Later, in a letter to Tanya, Tolstoy wrote about his joy at the news of her pregnancy and the 'unpleasant feeling' he had during the long interval after the previous one. A trace of male jealousy, perhaps, but no doubt Tolstoy was expressing his deeply held beliefs.

Schopenhauer taught that love was the most powerful illusion in the human heart, necessary to veil the drive to procreate: 'Marriages from love are contracted in the interest of the species, not of individuals. It is true that persons concerned imagine they are advancing their own happiness; but their actual aim is one that is foreign to themselves, since it lies in the production of an individual.'[9] The Tolstoys procreated successfully. To Sofia's dismay, Leo was indifferent to babies, but started loving children when they became toddlers. Sofia was a good and caring mother but marital relations, with all the jealousy, 'scenes' and reconciliations, remained fragile and too dependent on the ebbs and flows of Leo's erotic desires. Scared at first by her husband's ardent sexuality, Sofia gradually learned to share his passion, as she confesses in her memoirs. For many years she probably remained a reasonably good bedmate for her insatiable husband. Unfortunately this did not make their life any easier.

Sofia in 1866.

In February 1871 Sofia gave birth to her fifth child, named Maria after Leo's mother. Both her pregnancy and delivery were extremely difficult and the doctors thought that another pregnancy could be life-threatening. Tolstoy adamantly refused even to consider any contraceptive measures that were for him abomination worse than death. In *Anna Karenina* the final degradation of the heroine happens not when she betrays her husband, or even when she leaves him and their son for a lover, but when she reverts to contraception in order to stay sexually attractive to Vronsky. The rejection of motherhood turns Anna into a drug addict and a psychopath. In the middle of the novel she had been on the verge of dying. Retrospectively, the reader is prompted to conclude that this would have been a better outcome for Anna. Sofia went on to deliver eight more children, but three babies born after Maria died early; Tolstoy's decision caused fissures that never healed completely.

Apart from his interest in pathologies of the modern family, Tolstoy had literary reasons to revert to a novel about adultery. He was an avid reader of Western prose; his diaries, letters and conversations record scores of references to contemporary British, French and German novelists of different calibre; most often, favourable ones. However, one name is conspicuously absent from the list: Tolstoy mentioned Flaubert rarely, most often negatively and avoided speaking about his main novel. The only exception confirms this tendency – in 1892 Tolstoy wrote to his wife that he had read *Madame Bovary* and found it to have 'considerable merits and good reasons to be esteemed by the French' (*cw*, LXXXIV, p. 138), offering both tongue-in-cheek praise and an awkward attempt to pretend he had not read the book before. Flaubert's masterpiece had appeared in Paris in 1856. In January 1857 the author was put on trial for immorality before being triumphantly acquitted a month later. When Tolstoy arrived in Paris, two weeks after the trial, the city was still in a state of uproar. Tolstoy spent time with Turgenev, who believed *Madame Bovary* to be the best creation 'in the whole world of literature'. There is little doubt that Tolstoy would have read the sensational novel.

Flaubert's book is the ideal expression and a fine example of the spirit of nineteenth-century realism. Impeccably objective and detached, full of stunningly accurate, detailed and recognizable descriptions, it traces with an iron logic the psychological transformation of a pious girl full of dim poetic hopes and aspirations into an adulterous wife, who squanders her husband's money on an unfaithful lover and is driven by the inevitability of ruin to a horrifying suicide. Flaubert meticulously avoids any comments or moralistic conclusions, letting the characters and events speak for themselves. Fifteen years later Tolstoy took up the gauntlet and gave his own version of love, adultery and suicide.

The first draft of *Anna Karenina*, written in 1873, was very preliminary in nature: the names of the characters, their appearance and details of their biographies varied, some parts of the text were not yet ready and the author filled the gaps with short notes explaining what he was planning to write. Still, unlike *War and Peace*, the outline of the plot as well as the relations between the characters were clear to him from the very beginning. Present are all three couples connected by two pairs of siblings – Anna and Alabin (Oblonsky) and Dolly and Kitty – and the love of both female protagonists, Anna and Kitty, for the same man. Tolstoy made an early decision to begin the novel with the crisis in the Oblonsky family and to end it with Anna's railway station suicide. In the beginning of 1872 Tolstoy deliberately went to see the deformed body of Anna Pirogova, the abandoned housekeeper and lover of a local landlord, who had thrown herself under a train. The stories of the two Annas have very little in common, but Tolstoy was struck by the horrifying symbolism of the accident.

The early draft also bore the strong imprint of Schopenhauer's particular strain of misogyny. For the German thinker, women were born exclusively for attracting males and childbearing; and, as a consequence of this reproductive function, inclined to search for a mate with whom they might more successfully procreate. Anna, in this version, is a lascivious animal, not so much morally corrupt as inherently immoral. The other characters see her as possessed by a 'devil', an evil force or, in Schopenhauerian terms, the will to live. When she gets pregnant by Udashev (Vronsky), Anna's wet eyes shine with happiness. As was by now his custom, Tolstoy made things more subtle and less straightforward as he rewrote the novel. If the 'will to live' or 'force of life', as Tolstoy called it in the epigraph to one of the chapters, is irresistible, how could one possibly blame Anna? She had been 'sacrificed' on the altar of sexuality through marriage and denied frequent pregnancies. In the interval between *War and Peace* and *Anna Karenina* Tolstoy had mastered ancient Greek in order to read the classics in the original. He had been planning to read Sophocles and Euripides to use their experience in his own dramas. Instead, he turned his second novel into a classical tragedy of fate. In the final text, Anna is not acquitted, but her descent into hell acquires tragic greatness.

The chronological and cultural gap between a contemporary reader and Russian high society in Tolstoy's time obscures the historical dislocation in the foundation of the plot. Anna's stigma is grossly exaggerated; by social standards of the time, her behaviour was, of course, scandalous, but hardly unprecedented or exceptional. Russian high society was rife with stories of adultery and civil marriage. Emperor Alexander II lived and fathered children with his mistress, Ekaterina Dolgorukaya. This caused consternation among conservatives, who consolidated their opposition around the empress (one of whose ladies-in-waiting was Alexandra Tolstoy) and the heir to the throne. Such an aristocratic Fronde had little chance of bucking the trend set by a modernizing autocrat. Victorian bourgeois morality did not take root in a country where the bourgeoisie was relatively weak and uninfluential.

Tolstoy's own married sister Maria had a daughter with her civil partner, the Swedish viscount Hector de Kleen. Maria's history was different from Anna's – she had left her husband because she was not willing to 'serve as a senior wife in his harem'.[10] She was soon abandoned by the viscount and felt deeply repentant of her sins, but she never became a pariah. Likewise, Sofia's sister Liza, who failed to charm Tolstoy in 1862, divorced her impotent husband and remarried after eight years of unconsummated family life at exactly the time when her brother-in-law was writing *Anna Karenina*.

In a scene symbolically set in a theatre, the murmur of gossip is transformed into a roar of public damnation by Anna's inner voice. Her inner demons define her predicament, driving her towards near madness and ultimately to tragedy. In the epigraph to the novel, 'Vengeance is mine and I'll repay,' Tolstoy quotes Paul's Epistle to the Romans, but it remains unclear whether the actual revenge in question is performed by the just God of the New Testament or the 'terrible and cynical deity' of sexuality. Following Rousseau, Tolstoy condemned the hypocrisy of those who practised the vices for which they blame Anna, but 'society' was guilty not of ruining her love, but of corrupting her soul. Vronsky's seduction of a married woman meets with universal approval. Vronsky's mother also initially welcomes this liaison; Tolstoy was obviously thinking of his dear aunt Toinette, who wished for him to have an affair with a well-born married woman, a badge of honour for a young noble male.

'Emma Bovary – c'est moi,' Flaubert famously said. Tolstoy could hardly have made the same claim for Anna, though he endowed her with a flame of carnal desire all too familiar to him. There is no doubt, however, that Tolstoy could have said this about Konstantin Levin, the most autobiographical character he ever produced. Levin's surname is derived from the author's first name: Lev. Tolstoy endowed Levin with his own biographical details, traits of character, ways of estate management, everyday habits and preferences, social views and a sense of an anxious spiritual quest – nearly everything apart from literary talent. He did not have much left for Vronsky, the ideal image of a man *comme il faut*.

Nevertheless, 'despite a marked difference between Vronsky and Levin' (*AK*, p. 637), Anna is able to discern in them 'that common trait, which caused Kitty to fall in love with them both'. This 'common trait' was that of Tolstoy, who divided himself between the two characters. In *War and Peace* the main female character is first enchanted by an impeccable officer, but then understands her true feelings. In *Anna Karenina*, Tolstoy goes further. In an episode that serves the same role as the decisive meeting between Pierre and Natasha in *War and Peace*, Levin falls in love with Anna. When he returns home, Kitty's hysterical outburst seems to be excessive, if taken at face value; nothing has actually happened that could threaten their marriage. Still, both Levin and the author know that Kitty is right.

The interrelationship between Levin and Anna's family stories is often seen through the prism of the first, proverbial sentence of the novel: 'All happy families resemble one another, but each unhappy family is unhappy in its own way' (*AK*, p. 1). The structure of the novel, however, as well as the meaning of the opening maxim, cannot be reduced to such a shallow contrast. 'It is well known that happy marriages are rare,' wrote Schopenhauer.[11] Tolstoy described two happy families, if entirely different ones, in the epilogue to *War and Peace* and after that lost all interest in this subject.

In one of the drafts of *Anna Karenina* he wrote: 'We like to imagine misfortune as something concentrated, as a fact that happened, while misfortune is never an event in life, it is life itself, the long life which is unhappy, life which preserves the attributes of happiness, when happiness and the meaning of life are lost' (*CW*, xx, p. 370). It is this existential despair that drives Levin, a 'happy and healthy family man' (*CW*, xx, p. 562), so close to suicide that he has to hide the rope and the gun from sight so as not to hang or shoot himself. Mutual devotion and numerous children protect Levin and Kitty from the utter destitution of Karenin and Anna, or semi-destitution of Oblonsky and Dolly, but they are 'unhappy in their own way'. Levin's final religious revelation has nothing to do with his family; and on the last page, he even decides not to tell Kitty about it.

Tolstoy never needed reminders that death was near and omnipresent, but the 1870s provided him with many particular occasions to reflect on this. The year 1873, when Tolstoy started the novel, brought news of the death of Dasha Kuzminskaya, Tanya's elder daughter and the darling of both families. This was followed several months later by the sudden death of Tolstoy's fourth son Peter at the age of seventeen months. Next year Tolstoy's beloved aunt Toinette, Tatiana Yergolskaya, passed away after a prolonged illness. Another aunt, Pelageya Yushkova, who took care of him in Kazan and who had lived at Yasnaya Polyana as a widow for several years, died in 1875. That year also witnessed the deaths of two more of Tolstoy's babies, Nikolai and Varvara: the former did not survive until his first birthday, the latter passed away shortly after she was born. Death encircled Tolstoy's novel from the railway accident at the beginning that serves as a portent for Anna's suicide at the end.

In his first major novel, specially devoted to war and with infinitely more characters, Tolstoy showed death much more often than in the second. In *War and Peace* death is a necessary part of life's eternal cycle. The deaths of old Prince Bolkonsky, Prince Andrei and Hélène allow for the marriages of both Nikolai and Maria and Pierre and Natasha, leading to the births of their numerous offspring. In the world of *Anna Karenina* death begets new deaths: Anna's suicide induces Vronsky to go to war hoping to end his life there, and the death of Levin's brother drives Levin to near suicidal despair, from which he is mysteriously saved only by the help of a religious peasant.

In February 1873 Tolstoy wrote to his cousin Alexandra that he had reread *War and Peace* for the new edition with a feeling of 'repentance and shame . . . not unlike what a man experiences when he sees the remains of an orgy in which he has taken part'. Still, he was 'consoled' by the fact that he 'was carried by this orgy heart and soul, and thought that nothing else mattered beside it' (*Ls*, I, p. 257). He also told Alexandra that he was 'on the point of writing something again', but the 'orgy' did not repeat itself. In August 1875, midway through his work on the novel, Tolstoy complained to Strakhov that he had to 'set down again . . . at dull, commonplace Anna Karenina and prayed to God [for] strength to get it off [his] hands as quickly as possible in order to clear a space' (*Ls*, I, p. 280). Two months later he told Fet that 'in order to work, it is necessary for scaffolding to be erected under your feet,' that for a long time he was idly 'sitting and waiting' (*Ls*, I, p. 281) for the scaffolding, but now he felt they are in place and could resume his work. He was struggling to believe in the importance of his enterprise.

No wonder Tolstoy's new novel lacked the 'elemental force' that stunned Fet in the previous one. He compensated for that with an unsurpassable mastery of form that made William Faulkner, himself not alien to the secrets of the genre, call *Anna Karenina* 'the best novel ever written'. In the draft of the introduction to *War and Peace*, Tolstoy insisted that he was not writing a novel and that 'Russians in general do not know how to write novels' (*wp*, p. 1087). Now he was challenging those who were inclined to take him too literally. Gone were the fascinating weaknesses of his first major narrative: irritatingly long digressions, unprepared transformations of the characters, illogical holes in the plot, such as the thirteen-month pregnancy of Prince Andrei's first wife. The existential horror that permeates the pages of *Anna Karenina* had to be finely balanced by the perfection of the text. The Russian educator Sergey Rachinsky, one of the few representatives of his profession who had admired Tolstoy's *ABC* and *The Primer*, wrote to

Tolstoy that *Anna Karenina* was composed of two magnificent, but hardly connected novels. Tolstoy responded that he was 'proud of the architecture – the arches have been constructed in such a way that it is impossible to see where the keystone is' (*Ls*, I, p. 311). Such a defence of one of his completed works was nearly unique in the tens of thousands of letters Tolstoy wrote.

In May 1873, when finishing the first rough draft, Tolstoy wrote to Fet that 'good and evil are only materials out of which beauty is made'. Waiting for Anna to appear in the study of Vronsky's house, Levin gazes at the 'wonderful picture on the wall':

> It was not a picture, but a living and charming woman with curly black hair, bare shoulders and arms, and a dreamy half-smile on her lips, covered with elegant down, looking at him victoriously and tenderly with eyes that troubled him. The only thing that showed she was not alive was that she was more beautiful than a living woman could be. (*AK*, p. 630)

When Anna enters she turns out to be 'less brilliant', but Levin fails to notice it as 'there was something about her, new and attractive, which was not in the portrait' (*AK*, p. 630). The world that Tolstoy created was falling apart, but it was inherently beautiful. The author depicted it always staying on the scaffolding, without detaching himself from it in the manner of Flaubert. The effect of absolute realism was achieved not because Tolstoy 'objectively' portrayed the development of his characters, but because he portrayed himself portraying his characters, thus guaranteeing that the picture was true to life.

Anna Karenina provoked the ire of radical critics. Nekrasov, possibly still reeling from his failure to acquire the rights for the manuscript, wrote that Tolstoy had 'proved with patience and talent that a woman, being a mother and a wife, should not engage herself in affairs with officers or courtiers',[12] attempting with an epigram to reduce Tolstoy's novel to nothing more than trivial moralizing. Another critic, Petr Tkachev, called the novel 'a newest epic of aristocratic amours'.[13] These predictable barbs could still not reduce the success of the book, which became evident immediately after the publication of the first instalments and only grew after that. Readers were eager to read instalments as they were published and to buy the book; Tolstoy expected the planned collected edition of his work that was to include *Anna Karenina* to bring a profit of more than 60,000 roubles. Many critics' assessments were also more glowing than anyone could have dared to expect.

Tolstoy should have been especially flattered by the praise of Dostoevsky, who had always interested him as one of the 'martyrs of 1848' and as a writer. Tolstoy had mixed views on his major novels, but considered *Notes from the House of the Dead* 'the best book in all modern literature, Pushkin included . . . sincere, natural and Christian' (*Ls*, II, p. 338). This quasi-documentary narrative raised a topic eternally close to Tolstoy's heart: the meeting between a noble intellectual and people from the lower classes, brought together in the morbid environment of a hard labour camp. In his review, Dostoevsky wrote that Tolstoy's novel is marked by 'depth and potency with a realism of artistic portrayal hitherto unknown in Russia' and asserted that the book was the ultimate answer to the question of what Russia can give to Europe (*AK*, pp. 760–61). The final part of the novel, with its denunciation of the Balkan war, left the militarist Dostoevsky profoundly disappointed.

Shortly after the completion of *Anna Karenina* Tolstoy wrote a letter to Turgenev asking for forgiveness, stating that he 'bore no hostility' towards his former friend and offering 'all the friendship he was capable of' (*Ls*, I, pp. 318–19). The letter could not have arrived at a more appropriate time. Turgenev's health as well as his creative energy were on the wane. He had gone out of fashion with the reading public and regarded promoting Russian literature in

Europe as his main mission. Tolstoy was his greatest asset. He cried on reading the letter and at the first possible occasion came to visit his old friend and foe at Yasnaya Polyana; they met five times in the remaining years of his life. Turgenev charmed Tolstoy's family with funny stories about Paris life and once even danced the cancan in front of his daughters. Contrary to his habits, Tolstoy did not argue or interrupt, but just recorded the event in the diary he had by then resumed: 'Turgenev – cancan. Sad' (*Ds*, p. 177).

Turgenev was initially not very receptive to both Tolstoy's major novels. He found 'truly magnificent pages (the race, the scything, the hunt)' in *Anna Karenina*, but on the whole found it 'sour' and 'smelling of Moscow, of incense, of old maidishness, of Slavophilism, aristocratism and so on' (*ak*, p. 748). Now he reversed his earlier opinions. In 1879 the first French translation of *War and Peace* was published in Paris. Turgenev possibly encouraged this enterprise and sent a letter full of glowing praise to Edmond About, the editor of the Parisian newspaper *xixe Siècle*. He called the novel 'a great work by a great writer and . . . genuine Russia' (*wp*, p. 1108). Turgenev also sent copies of the French edition to leading French critics and writers including, of course, his literary hero.

Flaubert was quick to respond. In his letter, which Turgenev copied to Tolstoy in January 1880, he criticized the author for repetitions and philosophizing, but his general impression was more than favourable. He found the book to be 'of the first order', noting the author's art and psychology, and passages 'worthy of Shakespeare', and confessed that during the long reading he could not contain himself from 'outcries of admiration' (*tp*, i, 192). The author of *Madame Bovary* died the same year and did not have a chance to read *Anna Karenina* as its French translation appeared only in 1885.

Tolstoy's reaction to this new level of recognition is unknown. Most likely he was unfazed. At first, relieved from the burden of

Anna Karenina, he was contemplating a return to his earlier literary plans, albeit radically revised: the novels about Peter the Great and the Decembrists. The former took the shape of an epic narrative provisionally entitled *A Hundred Years*, which was to unfold simultaneously in parallel settings at court and in a peasant hut, covering the whole period from the birth of the modernizing tsar up to the beginning of the reign of Alexander I in 1801. The latter was to deal with the aftermath of the 1825 rebellion, when the former conspirators encountered the people they had hoped to liberate in Siberian exile. When added to the already completed *War and Peace* and *Anna Karenina*, these works would have amounted to a tetralogy stretching over two centuries of national history.

These plans soon ran into the ground. The historic philosophy of *War and Peace* implied that the acts of the ruler reflect the cumulative will of the nation; and thus Peter's victory meant that he was on the right side of history. Tolstoy no longer believed that. The more he studied the period, the more the great reformer seemed to him a 'debauched syphilitic' (*cw*, xxxv, p. 552) beheading his subjects with his own hands out of purely sadistic pleasure, as he described the Westernizing tsar a quarter of a century later. Already in 1870, reading *The History of Russia* by the eminent Russian historian Sergei Solovyev, Tolstoy remarked in his notebook:

Reading how they plundered, ruled, fought, devastated (history speaks only about this), you can't help thinking – what did they plunder? And from this question to another one: who produced what they plundered? Who and how made bread for everyone? Who caught the black foxes and sables they gave as presents to ambassadors, who extracted gold and iron, who bred the horses, oxen, rams, who built the houses and palaces, who transported the goods? Who bore and brought up these people of the same root? . . . Among the functions of the people's life there is this necessity to have the people plundering, devastating, bathing in luxury and bullying. And those are the rulers – the miserable ones who have to renounce anything human in them. (*cw*, XLVIII, p. 124)

At that time Tolstoy still believed that a ruling class, however repulsive, was a necessity in the course of history. Nearly a decade later he could no longer see any justification for their plundering and bullying. Writing the history of a nation was one thing, but writing the history of a criminal gang was totally different. By the same token, if a peasant family was not, as he had previously believed, mysteriously connected with events in the palace, its story was that of a victim, rather than a historical actor. Tolstoy knew his job too well not to understand that this approach would not sustain a narrative stretching over a century. The story of the exiled Decembrists also lost its allure. The dialogue between the nobles and the peasants he envisaged became useless, because the educated classes had nothing to teach or even to say to those who worked on the land. The only useful thing the ruling elite could do was simply to disappear and let the suffering people lead their own life according to their own ideals and values.

In April 1878, three months after the publication of the complete text of *Anna Karenina*, Tolstoy wrote to Strakhov that everything seemed to be ready for him to start writing – and fulfilling his earthly mission. The only thing he was lacking was 'the push of belief . . . in the importance of the occupation . . . the energy of delusion, that earthly elemental energy that could not be invented' (*cw*, LXII, pp. 410–11). The 'energy of delusion' that had previously sustained him stemmed from a belief that his writing would change the world or, no less importantly, himself. When working on *War and Peace* that energy was burning in him; when he wrote *Anna Karenina* its intensity became more subdued, but he still managed to keep it alive. Now there was no literary plan that could spark that delusion.

In his *Confession*, written in 1879 and published in 1882, Tolstoy gave a concise description of how his life was brought to a virtual standstill by a simple question he asked himself many times: "'Very well; you will be more famous than Gogol or Pushkin or Shakespeare or Molière, or than all the writers in the world – and what of it?" And I could find no reply at all' (*cw*, XXIII, p. 11).

3

A Lonely Leader

The last page of *Anna Karenina* describes Levin's religious epiphany. The conversion of the hero of the novel roughly coincided with that of the author. As he approached the end of his narrative, Tolstoy came to the conviction that only God could restore meaning to the world permeated with death.

In his *Confessions* Tolstoy portrayed himself as a sceptic, an atheist even, who had finally recognized the futility of earthly pursuits such as fame and prosperity. His diaries tell a different story. The hope of a religious awakening was Tolstoy's long-cherished dream, something he had thought about and wrestled with for decades. In June 1851 Tolstoy recorded in his diary that he was fighting with the 'petty, vicious side of life', and asked God 'to receive him into His bosom'. The 'sweetness of the feeling' this prayer gave him was 'impossible to express' (*Ds*, p. 26). Another time Tolstoy confessed that, while he could not prove God's existence to himself, he 'believed in Him' and asked Him for help 'to understand Him' (*Ds*, p. 59).

The characters of his novels also experience spiritual epiphanies: Prince Andrei gazing into the sky of Austerlitz and preparing for his death, and Pierre embracing the teaching of the Freemasons and when in French captivity. Anna Karenina and her husband feel the raptures of Christian forgiveness as Anna lies on what seems to be her deathbed. With the evident exception of Andrei's final revelation, however, these existential experiences are, as the

Russian writer and thinker Lydia Ginzburg has put it, 'reversible'.[1] They cannot change the lives of the characters, who later revert to their old ways. Tolstoy suggests, however, that Levin's newly found beliefs are different.

In 1873, the year he began writing *Anna Karenina*, Tolstoy wrote to the atheist Fet about the necessity of 'religious respect'. Despite his contempt for 'religious rites', Tolstoy's brother Sergei had ordered an Orthodox funeral for a deceased child. Both brothers had 'the feeling almost of revulsion at this ritualism', but Leo had to confess that he could not imagine any alternatives:

> What could my brother have done to carry the decomposing body of his child out of his house at the end? . . . And where should it be put, how should it be buried? What, generally speaking, is a fitting way to end things? Is there anything better than a requiem, incense etc.? (I, at least, can't think of anything.) And what about growing weak and dying? Should one wet oneself, s..., and nothing more? That's no good.
>
> I would like to give outward expression to the gravity and importance, the solemnity and the religious awe in the presence of the greatest event in life of every human being. And I can think of nothing more fitting – and fitting for all ages and all stages of development – than a religious setting. (*Ls*, I, p. 256)

Deaths of close family members moved Tolstoy from 'religious respect' to sincere belief. Like Levin, he expected spiritual guidance from the peasants working his land. It only followed that he was eager to accept the religion that supported them in their toils and freed them from fear and anguish of their mortality.

Tolstoy immersed himself in Orthodoxy with characteristic fervour. He fasted and patiently stood during long liturgies, bowing and praying on his knees. He made a pilgrimage to Kiev, the cradle of Russian Christianity, to see relics of the first Russian saints.

He visited monasteries to talk to leading clergymen. Especially important was his pilgrimage to Optina Pustyn', the monastery famous for its elders, who provided spiritual nourishment to many believers including Dostoevsky, who described Optina in *The Brothers Karamazov*. Tolstoy had long conversations with Amvrosii, the most revered elder of the monastery, the prototype for Dostoevsky's Zosima. Wishing to read the Gospels in the original, Tolstoy immersed himself in studies of theological literature and biblical Greek.

The longer and harder he studied traditional Orthodoxy, however, the less he felt able to believe in it. As he wrote in his *Confessions*, he 'had envied the peasants for their illiteracy and their lack of education', but their unquestioning faith was beyond his reach:

> I was listening to an illiterate peasant, a pilgrim, talking about God, faith, life, and salvation, and a knowledge of faith was opened up to me. I grew closer to the people as I listened to their reflections on life and faith, and I began to understand the truth more and more . . . But as soon as I mixed with learned believers or picked up their books, a certain doubt, dissatisfaction and bitterness over their arguments rose up within me, and I felt that the more I grasped their discourses, the further I strayed from the truth and the closer I came to the abyss. (*CW*, XXIII, p. 52)

From his early days, Tolstoy had been certain that God endowed human beings with sufficient reason and moral feeling to see the truth. True religion did not need numerous dogmas or the traditional Church; it had to be self-evident, simple and clear. Historic Christianity, rooted in mysteries that one had to believe but could never fully comprehend, did not satisfy him. The sheer number of Christian denominations and fierce theological debates between them was proof, in Tolstoy's eyes, that none of the existing churches preserved the spirit of the Gospels. Tolstoy's break with Orthodoxy was the result of tortuous inner reflection, but, as was always the case with him, appeared quick and decisive: at a dinner during one of the fasts, he suddenly asked his son to pass him a meatball prepared for the non-fasting members of the household.

Already during the siege of Sebastopol in 1855 Tolstoy had felt himself 'capable of devoting' his entire life to the realization of a 'great' and 'stupendous' idea – the creation of 'a new religion appropriate to the stage of development of mankind – the religion of Christ, but purged of mysticism, a practical religion not promising future bliss but giving bliss on earth'. The young officer aspired to work 'consciously . . . towards the union of mankind by religion' (*Ds*, p. 87). By the age of fifty, and great novels behind him, Tolstoy found himself ready to embark on that mission. He aspired to refute nearly 2,000 years of errors, self-deceit and outright lies and to present to the world the real, unadulterated word of Christ.

This mission went beyond the reformation or purification of existing Christianity. The mantle of Martin Luther was too tight for Tolstoy. He wanted to bring to the world a new faith based on some parts of the Gospels, especially the Sermon on the Mount, while totally rejecting other major parts of the New Testament, such as the Acts of the Apostles or the Book of Revelation, and such basic dogmas as the Immaculate Conception, the Holy Trinity and the Resurrection.

Between 1879 and 1882 Tolstoy produced the major theological trilogy that he intended to serve as the foundation of 'a religion of Christ purged of beliefs and mysticism'. In *Confessions* he traced his personal evolution from the instinctive religiosity of childhood, through the debauchery and dissipation of youth, the literary and managerial pursuits of his married years, through excruciating despair, acceptance and then renunciation of Orthodoxy before finally arriving at an understanding of the eternal and simple truths of religion that brought him long-sought spiritual peace.

In his *Critique of Dogmatic Theology* Tolstoy set out a theoretical refutation of the doctrine of the Russian Orthodox Church as expounded in the Orthodox Dogmatic Theology of Archbishop Makarii, the accepted canonical source of dogma in nineteenth-century Russian Orthodoxy. He also prepared a new annotated translation of the Gospels followed by a digest, *The Gospels in Brief*, as it is known in English.

Having completed this tripartite demolition of the edifice of historical Christianity, Tolstoy moved on to making a positive exposition of the new faith. In the years 1883–4 he wrote his groundbreaking treatise *What I Believe*. Over five years he had developed a comprehensive religious, moral, political, social and economic philosophy that was stunning in its logic and consistency. It is easy to reject Tolstoy's teachings in their entirety, but to unpick them and juxtapose one part against another to show inner contradictions is incredibly difficult, if not impossible. Tolstoy found his faith in the Gospels, but interpreted them in a way that resonated with thoughts and feelings he had cherished all his life. His Christ was divine not because he had been conceived by the Holy Spirit and risen from the dead, but because his words and life were the absolute embodiment of God's wisdom and goodness in a way that was naturally consistent with simple reason and eternal morality:

> The doctrine of Christ is the doctrine of truth, and, therefore, faith in Christ is not a trust in anything that refers to Jesus, but a knowledge of the truth. It is impossible to persuade or bribe a man to fulfil it. He who understands the doctrine of Christ will have faith in Him, because His doctrine is truth. He who knows the truth cannot refuse to believe in it. (*cw*, xxiii, p. 410)

Tolstoy read the Gospels as the story of a poor bastard boy and homeless vagabond who willingly gave his life for the light he brought to the world. The prophet's humble origins and his shameful death did not diminish the glory and beauty of his word; on the contrary, they gave it a power that could only be undermined by improbable claims of a genealogical descent from the Creator or an artificial happy-end-like Resurrection. The idea that God could have willingly sent his son to the cross sounded to Tolstoy like a blasphemy.

According to Tolstoy, the 'doctrine of Christ' consisted of five commandments supplementing, correcting or cancelling the commandments of Moses. The first one was never to condemn anyone or regard anyone as an outlaw. The second was not to commit adultery, which included divorce and remarriage. The third was not to swear oaths, that is, never to pledge loyalty to earthly governments or to participate in legal proceedings. The fourth commandment, and key in Tolstoy's eyes, was not to resist evil with violence. Even in life-threatening circumstances one should not resort to force, but instead accept one's fate with humility and prayer. Finally, the fifth commandment was not to regard other human beings as enemies or aliens, thus abolishing the division of mankind into nations.

Tolstoy's starting point was the opening sentences of Rousseau's *Social Contract*: 'Man is born free; and everywhere he is in chains. One thinks himself the master of others, and still remains a greater slave than they.' Rousseau's thoughts were echoed by the authors of the Declaration of Independence, who aspired to establish an institutional framework that could preserve and guarantee natural liberty. As was always the way with Tolstoy, his conclusions were more radical than others had dared to conceive. For him, the divinely ordained nature of equality meant that no form of coercion could ever be legitimate and no violence could ever be justified. Tolstoy insisted on a literal interpretation of these precepts. He did not envisage an ideal Christian state, because any state with its monarchs, parliaments, politicians, laws, courts, prisons, soldiers, judges, bureaucrats, tax collectors and so on presupposed the existence of a hierarchy and the exercise of power by some over others.

In *War and Peace* Tolstoy glorified popular resistance to invasion; now he regarded military service as one of the worst abominations in human history. Native government was no more legitimate than any foreign one; living under the rule of the French, the Turks or whoever else would be a lesser evil for his compatriots than going to war and killing people. Equally, no crime could ever justify violent punishment. Robbers and murderers acting at their own risk deserved more compassion than executioners or judges who send people to the gallows protected by the law and the repressive apparatus of the state. In general, mortals were not entitled to make laws, all they had to do was to obey the eternal rules of God, but even those should not be enforced, as the Church hierarchy and coercion in the sphere of religious beliefs were especially repulsive.

A. N. Wilson, the author of a perceptive biography of Tolstoy, called this anarchist credo 'the silliest' and 'the least Russian' thing Tolstoy ever said.[2] The question of 'silliness' of Tolstoy's worldview is, of course, fully dependent upon the perspective of the biographer, but the claim of its 'un-Russianness' is plainly wrong.

Tolstoy was a contemporary and a compatriot of such leading figures in the history of European anarchism as Mikhail Bakunin and Piotr Kropotkin. All three of them were aristocratic intellectuals who looked for ideals in the life of Russian peasant communes, in the stubborn resistance of sectarians and Old Believers to the official Church and central authorities, in Cossack settlements providing military support to the crown, but defying state bureaucracy in their way of life. No less important for Tolstoy were the numberless wanderers, pilgrims and beggars who left their homes and villages to search for God. The utopian vision of life without a state, masters or an official Church is no less important for Russian intellectual tradition and popular aspirations than its antithesis: unswerving trust in the secular and spiritual authorities. Tolstoy and Dostoevsky represented the two trends.

In 1881 Dostoevsky met Tolstoy's cousin Alexandra and asked her to explain to him 'the new direction taken by Lev Nikolaevich'. Fervently Orthodox, Alexandra regarded Dostoevsky as a prophet. She prepared for him copies of several of Tolstoy's letters and, at his request, read them out to him. Dostoevsky listened, 'his hands on his head repeating in a desperate voice: "It's all wrong".' According to Alexandra Tolstoy, 'he did not sympathize with a single thought of Lev Nikolaevich' (*LNT & AAT*, p. 32). Intending to write a refutation, he took home with him both the copies and the originals.

Given Tolstoy's taste for heated debates, a letter from Dostoevsky could have provoked one of the most fascinating dialogues in literary history. As it happened, Dostoevsky died five days later and his polemical answer to Tolstoy remained unwritten. The letters he borrowed from Alexandra Tolstoy disappeared forever.

Tolstoy wrote to Strakhov shortly afterwards:

I never saw the man and never had any direct relations with him, and suddenly when he died, I realized that he was the closest, dearest and most necessary man for me. I was a writer and all writers are vain and envious – I at least was that sort of writer. But it never occurred to me to measure myself against him, never. Everything that he did (every good and real thing that he did) was such, that the more he did it, the happier I was. Art arouses envy in me and so does intelligence, but the things of the heart arouse only joy. I always considered him my friend, and I never thought otherwise than that we should meet, and that it was my fault that we hadn't managed to do so yet. And suddenly during dinner – I was late and dining alone – I read that he was dead. Some support gave way under me. I was overcome; but then it became clear how precious he was to me, and I cried and am still crying. (*Ls*, ii, p. 340)

He was fully aware of the differences between his and Dostoevsky's views, but he also knew that they both understood that the world around them was crumbling and believed that their duty was to prevent it. Now he felt that he had to shoulder the burden and the responsibility alone.

For twenty years Tolstoy's main preoccupations were novels and family life. In 1881 the need to educate his eldest children compelled him to buy a house in Moscow. In the meantime, his country changed beyond recognition. The abolition of serfdom, rapid industrialization and a demographic boom had unleashed a flood of migrants from the villages to the cities. Railroads enabled massive grain exports that had the effect of pushing up bread prices. The peasants, though liberated from serfdom, could not benefit from this increasing demand because most agricultural land remained in the hands of their former landlords, and the rents rose more steeply than profits from harvests. The land owned by peasants belonged to rural communes and was regularly

View from the garden of Tolstoy's house in Moscow, 1898.

redistributed between households according to the size of their families. This meant that individual peasants could not sell their land before moving to the city and had little incentive to invest in it to increase productivity. Social changes and the generational imbalance caused by the demographic boom were destroying traditional ways of life and family structures. Crime, drunkenness and prostitution were on the rise both in villages and cities. Tolstoy could now witness the new urban poverty at first hand. The poorest could not rely on the kind of social network provided by rural communes. Their extreme misery and moral degradation was made even more abject and manifest by the stunning economic growth that had belatedly begun in the 1880s.

Social crisis brought political unrest. The Great Reforms had boosted the expectations of the growing number of young, active and eager graduates churned out by a proliferating number of universities. A highly stratified society could barely accommodate them or enable them to improve their social status, leading to frustration. Radical groups began a campaign of revolutionary propaganda among the peasants. When this strategy failed they turned to outright terror. The second half of the 1870s was marked by several unsuccessful attempts on the life of Alexander ii before the assassins finally succeeded on 1 March 1881, the day before a decree establishing a proto-parliamentary representative body with consultative functions was due to be signed by the reforming tsar. The assassination ushered in a backlash led by the new emperor Alexander iii and Konstantin Pobedonostsev, an arch-reactionary whose influence expanded beyond his original role of supervising Church policy and came to define the spirit of the new reign.

Tolstoy had some sympathy for the revolutionaries. He appreciated the power of their convictions, their readiness for martyrdom and sincere compassion for the poor, qualities that, in his view, were entirely wanting in the kind of educated society in which he lived. At the same time, he was appalled by their narrow-mindedness, atheism and positivism, and most of all by their willingness to resort to violence, based on the obstinate belief that they knew the needs of the people they intended to liberate better than those people themselves. From the early 1880s Tolstoy was certain that revolution was approaching and had no doubt that the regime that would emerge from the ruins would be even more tyrannical than the existing one.

He wrote a letter to Pobedonostsev petitioning the new tsar to pardon his father's assassins. Tolstoy argued that such a pardon would demonstrate moral greatness and Christian feelings and engender a process of reconciliation in society. Both Pobedonostsev and Alexander III refused to consider such an act of clemency that, in their eyes, would be tantamount to encouraging political terror. The new emperor admired Tolstoy as a writer, but began to view his activities as subversive.

In January 1882, hoping to understand the roots of social evil and ways in which it might be alleviated more deeply, Tolstoy volunteered to take part in conducting the census. He chose one of the most notorious parts of Moscow, full of shelters for the homeless and the outcast. He spoke to people, listened to their life stories and gave out significant amounts of money. For a while Tolstoy sought to advance plans for a charity that would collect money by subscription and administer the relief. This venture failed. The rich were not interested in providing the required funds and the poor themselves tended to spend the money Tolstoy gave them on drinking, gambling and fornication.

Charity was not an answer, but Tolstoy could never accept the idea that any problem was completely insoluble. He spent several years working on an essay in which he tried to apply his new religious views to practical social issues. The title *What then Must We Do?* openly echoed that of Chernyshevsky's banned novel *What Is to Be Done?*, in which the main female character organized cooperatives among working-class girls, often real or potential prostitutes, and managed to put their lives back on track. Chernyshevsky did not doubt that given support, guidance and education, the poor would rationally choose what was more beneficial for them.

Tolstoy knew better. He spent time and money researching the reactions of the destitute to the patronizing help of intellectuals. He soon learned that while small gifts, commonly of two or three kopecks, were met with a sort of ritual gratitude, attempts to donate significant sums only provoked animosity and resentment towards the benefactor. The poor interpreted excessive generosity as a paternalistic attempt to subjugate them to the rules and discipline of a society they rejected. Anger and cheating served as perverse means to defend their human dignity.

In his essay Tolstoy proceeded from his own first-hand experience of big city misery to address the problems of division of labour, the nature of money, property, taxation and so on. The structure of his argument was rambling and even included a detailed history of Britain's colonization of the islands of Fiji, but his conclusions were clear and straightforward. He was convinced that the lifestyle of the leisured classes, centred on artificial needs and dependent upon taxation and property rights, brought destitution to working people and could only be sustained through coercive institutions like the army, the courts and the police.

A social and political order based on violence and injustice was rapidly losing the air of legitimacy it had once held in the eyes of the oppressed. The only way for the rich to avoid imminent catastrophe was to renounce privilege and go back to manual labour, a natural life and the eternal principles of Christian morality. The nineteenth century had seen many refutations of modernity, but no other mainstream thinker had dared to be so uncompromising.

As far as Tolstoy was concerned, no idea, belief or conviction had any value unless it shaped personal behaviour. It took him several years to overhaul his lifestyle completely, but he was constantly

Ilya Repin, *Leo Tolstoy Ploughing*, 1887, oil on card.

making changes. He began working in the fields, wearing peasant clothes and grew a peasant-style beard that was easier to take care of. He reverted to simple food, gradually becoming a complete vegetarian, stopped smoking and drinking and renounced the hunting that had once been his favourite sport. He explained each step in a passionate article. Tolstoy dismissed his personal servants and started to bring water to the house, cut wood and clean his room. The most difficult thing to get used to, by his own admission, was taking out and washing his chamber pot, but he did that too. He also renounced financial transactions and carried only small amounts of cash for the needy. Arguably the most eccentric of his new preoccupations was shoemaking, something he engaged in with such real passion that every success in the craft caused childlike happiness.

Tolstoy's behaviour provoked in people who surrounded him emotions that ranged from mild amusement to outright indignation. Fet ordered a pair of boots, insisted on paying six roubles and provided an invoice with a pledge to wear them regularly. Most likely, he did not keep his promise. The boots are still on display in the Tolstoy museum in Moscow and do not look worn out. As an atheist, conservative and aesthete, Fet could not approve the 'new direction' taken by his friend.

Turgenev's feelings were stronger. In June 1883, as he readied himself for death, Turgenev wrote a farewell letter to Tolstoy. Too weak to hold a pen, he scribbled with a pencil:

> I cannot recover – there is no use thinking of it. I am writing to you particularly to tell you how glad I am to have been your contemporary and to express to you my last, sincere request. My friend, return to literary activity! That gift came to you from whence come all the rest. Ah, how happy I should be, if I could think that my request would have an impact on you!! . . . My friend, great writer of the Russian land, heed my request. Let me know if you receive this bit of paper, and permit me once more to embrace you heartily, heartily and your wife and all yours. I can't write more, too tired. (*TP*, p. 203)

He died two months later. Tolstoy was moved deeply enough to agree, in spite of his hatred of public ceremonies, to give a speech at Turgenev's commemoration in Moscow. The appearance of Tolstoy's name in the announcement made the authorities ban the event altogether. At the same time this final manifestation of Turgenev's desire to guide him and his excessive rhetorical flourish irritated Tolstoy. Much later he repeated the formula 'the great writer of the Russian land', sarcastically adding 'and what about water?'[3] Still, he partially 'heeded' Turgenev's request. After several years he resumed writing prose, but always regarded this as being subordinate to his role as a moral and religious preacher.

The people who were most alarmed by Tolstoy's evolution were the members of his family. In May 1881, in the wake of the riots and

Jewish pogroms that followed the assassination of Alexander II, Tolstoy recorded his impression of one family conversation:

> Seryozha [Sergei, his eldest son] said: 'Christ's teaching is well known, but it is difficult'. I said: 'You would not say it is difficult to run out of a blazing room through the only door . . .' They began to talk. Hanging is necessary, flogging is necessary, to prevent the people from rioting – that would be terrible. But hitting Jews – that's not a bad thing. Then without rhyme or reason, they talked about fornication and with relish. Somebody is mad – either them or me. (*Ds*, p. 175)

Two months later he was appalled by an 'enormous dinner with champagne' at which all the Tolstoy and Kuzminsky children wore belts that cost the equivalent of a month's salary for the hungry and overworked peasants around them. He discussed it with Tatiana Kuzminsky, who used to understand him better than others. After that he contemplated 'until morning' about his irreparable rift with the people who were so close to him, writing in despair, 'They are not human beings' (*Ds*, pp. 176–7).

His wife was the main culprit. She was accustomed to shifts in his 'fickle opinions', but this crisis threatened the very foundations of her life. Initially Sofia was inclined to interpret it in line with her old fears. After one of their quarrels in 1882, she recorded in her diary that, for the first time in twenty years of living under one roof, Leo had spent the night in a different bed. She was convinced that if he would not come to her, it meant that he loved another woman. Finally he appeared and they reconciled in the usual way. Sofia came to realize that her family problems were not caused by other women, but that did not make her any happier or less jealous.

The couple's ensuing quarrels and misunderstandings soon became public, engendering divisions among Tolstoy's admirers that are still alive today. Some blame Sofia, who refused to 'follow' her great husband in his spiritual quest, thus turning their lives into an everyday hell. Others exonerate her. She was responsible for the well-being of eight children (as Tolstoy's religious convictions evolved, she had given birth to three more sons, Andrei in 1877, Mikhail in 1879 and Alexei, who later died at the age of four, in 1881) and could ill afford to accommodate the whims of the genius. In truth, however, the roots of this family tragedy went deeper.

Married at the age of eighteen, Sofia felt a sense of mission no less important than that of Leo's. While he had renounced his previous life to become a great writer, she had done the same in order to become the wife of a great writer. Copying the manuscripts of *War and Peace*, she recorded her nearly religious attitude to his art:

It is great delight for me. Morally, I am experiencing the whole world of impressions and thoughts by copying the novel. Nothing affects me as strongly as his thoughts and his talent. It started to happen not long ago. Did I change myself or is the novel really so good – I can't tell. I write quickly enough to follow the novel and slowly enough to grasp all the interest, think over, feel and discuss his every thought. We often speak about the novel and he for some reason (which makes me proud) listens to my thoughts and strongly believes in them. (*SAT-DS*, p. 80)

Twenty years later, in October 1886, she reacted to his profound and intimate thoughts in a very different way:

I often wonder why Levochka puts me in the position of always being guilty without guilt. Because he wants me not to live, but to suffer all the time looking at the poverty, sickness and misfortunes of the people, and wants me to seek them if I do not meet them in my life. This is what he demands from the children as well. Is it necessary?

. . . If you meet such a person in the course of your life, help him, but why search for him? (*SAT-DS*, p. 112).

One can discern here not only a criticism of Tolstoy's ethical theories, but a clear feeling that her husband's sympathy for the poor undermined her status in his life. She belonged to the world of his novels and his rejection of prose challenged her own perception of her identity and mission of 'a writer's wife who takes our authorial business close to heart' – as she once put it in a letter to her sister.[4]

Tolstoy's new philosophy valued universal love for humankind above 'exclusive love' for the objects of personal commitment. In his translation of the Gospels he summarized the relevant lines from Luke and Matthew as 'For those who understood my teachings neither father, nor mother, wife or children or property would have any meaning.' Tolstoy saw the absolute embodiment of 'exclusive love' in sexuality. The Christian ideal demanded total chastity. Even if original sin could be partially redeemed by procreation, it remained immoral not only outside the family, but within it as well.

Until late in his life Tolstoy felt carnal desires for his wife, but always regarded them as a sign of weakness he was unable to overcome. Sofia repeatedly wrote in her diary and autobiography that after their most passionate lovemaking Lev became cold and detached. In 1908, before his eightieth birthday, he complained in the 'secret diary' that his multiple biographies would not discuss his 'attitude to the seventh commandment': 'Although I have never once been unfaithful to my wife, I have experienced loathsome, criminal desire for her. Nothing of this will appear and ever appears in biographies. And this is very important' (*Ds*, p. 423).

Tolstoy knew that after his death his diary could become available to his wife and even be made public, yet there is no reason to doubt his claim of being always faithful to his wife. He was never shy about blaming himself for actual or imaginable sins.

Once, in 1879, he was close to succumbing to temptation. Heading for an encounter with a house cook, Domna, he was stopped by his son, who asked him for help with his lessons. Tolstoy was certain that divine intervention had saved him, but for a while he lost confidence in his strength to resist the Devil. He asked Vasily Alekseev, the tutor of his children, to accompany him all the time to avoid falling into the abyss. Five years later he described the same episode in detail in a repentant letter to Vladimir Chertkov.

It is notable that the maniacally jealous and suspicious Sofia never accused him of adultery in her own diaries, even though they were full of bitter and venomous reproaches. In her memoirs, written with the specific goal of settling scores with her husband and listing all his offences against her, she wrote that not a single time in her life had she experienced his infidelity. Still, she could not reconcile herself to the role of necessary evil she had to play in her husband's moral universe. She refused to 'follow' Tolstoy, because she knew that he was not calling her anywhere.

Rumours about Tolstoy's new religious beliefs spread quickly. Scores of visitors eager to discuss God, morality, life and love with the most famous Russian writer flocked to Yasnaya Polyana and Tolstoy's Moscow house in Khamovniki. Most of them were peasants disillusioned with the official Church, persecuted sectarians, self-appointed prophets, wanderers and mystics – 'the dark ones', as Sofia contemptuously called them. Both Sofia and Alexandra Tolstoy wrote about Vasily Siutaev, a peasant from the Tver region, who preached in favour of fraternal relations among people, denied the division of property, condemned church rituals and educational institutions and exerted influence on the author of *War and Peace*.

The most important visitor Tolstoy ever received, however, came from his own social milieu. Vladimir Chertkov belonged to the cream of the Russian aristocracy and was exceptionally rich. As an officer in an elite guards regiment he had led a dissipated life,

Vasily Siutaev (the first 'dark one'), 1880s.

but suddenly repented and engaged himself in the education of peasants and charitable work. He had spent time in England, where he became close to the British evangelicals. When he came to see Tolstoy for the first time in 1883, Chertkov was 29: the remaining 53 years of his life, half before and half after Tolstoy's death, were wholly dedicated to the dissemination of Tolstoy's work and the popularization of his teachings. He became Tolstoy's closest friend and most devoted and trusted disciple.

Portrait of Vladimir
Chertkov by Mikhail
Nesterov, 1890.

At first, Sofia was well disposed to Chertkov – at least he was
not a 'dark one'. This mild sympathy, however, soon turned into
suspicious resentment and later into intense hatred. She had finally
found the most appropriate object for her jealousy. She blamed
Chertkov for her estrangement from her husband, even though she
knew well enough that her family life had already reached breaking
point before Chertkov made an appearance. Several months before
Lev's death, Sofia discovered in his diary for 1851 an entry in which
he confessed that he had always loved men more than women. She
openly accused her 82-year-old husband of having homosexual
relations with Chertkov.

This accusation, based on a statement written nearly sixty years
earlier, in which the diarist himself expressed a 'terrible aversion'
towards homosexuality, was utterly irrational. Yet in a perverse way
Sofia was perhaps on to something. The handsome, aristocratic,
self-confident Chertkov matched a masculine ideal so successfully
described in Tolstoy's great novels. Vladimir could play Prince

Andrei to the somewhat Bezukhovian Lev, never sure of himself, hesitant and prone to scorching self-introspection. Traumatized by the alienation of his elder sons, Tolstoy saw in Chertkov his true spiritual son and heir. At the same time, notwithstanding the difference in age, Chertkov assumed from the very beginning the role of the paternal figure Tolstoy had lacked in his teenage years. The teacher could always confess to his pupil the most intimate movements of his heart, his doubts and fears and be certain to receive clear and definite answers.

Chertkov was also highly efficient. On Tolstoy's advice, he organized a publishing house called 'Intermediary', specializing in cheap editions for the masses. The bulk of its output consisted of popular stories, tales and essays written, edited or recommended by Tolstoy. The rendering of folk tales and composing moral and religious parables for 'Intermediary' allowed Tolstoy to satisfy a need for artistic creativity without compromising his renunciation of literature. Some of these stories, such as *What Men Live By* or *How Much Land Does a Man Need?*, show that his literary genius had not left him.

Still Tolstoy aspired to produce a work for the educated reader that would be both as psychologically convincing and profound as *Anna Karenina*, and as dry and didactically unambiguous as his *Primer*. He achieved this synthesis in *The Death of Ivan Ilyich*. Tolstoy felt that he had to apologize for this endeavour, as he wrote to Chertkov, 'I promised to finish this for my wife to include in her new edition, but this article only relates to our circle in its form . . . in content it relates to everyone' (*Ls*, ii, p. 383). Sofia found the story 'a bit morbid, but very good' (*cw*, xxvi, p. 681), and eagerly included it in the twelfth volume of Tolstoy's collected works. She still hoped that her husband would return to literature and that this would save their family.

The Death of Ivan Ilyich is a painfully naturalistic depiction of the agonies of a high-ranking official dying from cancer. Contemporary doctors admired the precision with which Ivan Ilyich's symptoms were described and were able to diagnose not only the nature of the illness, but the exact location of the tumour and the phases of its progress. Of course, depicting the physiology of dying was not the true focus of Tolstoy's attention. He was writing about the most important problem he had ever encountered.

The 'Arzamas horror' that afflicted Tolstoy in 1869 had taught him that the presence of death can render life meaningless. A successful career, an outwardly functional family life, refined tastes and a dignified lifestyle had made Ivan Ilyich proud of himself, but on his deathbed he has no significant memories to sustain him. His illness starts from a bruise he gets arranging fashionable furniture in his apartment. At the end of his life he feels completely alienated from his wife, children, friends and colleagues, and no one, except his servant, really sympathizes with his demise and tries in earnest to understand his needs and alleviate his pain.

The final turn of the narrative, however, brings Ivan Ilyich closer to Prince Andrei than to Anna Karenina. Pity for his schoolboy son, who bursts into tears and kisses his hand, and for his wife, who stands nearby with tears in her eyes, opens the way for him to feel universal love that melts both the fear of death and death itself. Instead of sucking meaning out of life, death retrospectively endows it with a higher purpose.

> Suddenly it grew clear to him that what had been
> oppressing him, and would not leave him, was all
> dropping away at once, from two sides, from ten sides,
> from all sides. He was sorry for them, he must act so as
> not to hurt them: release them and free himself from these
> sufferings. 'How good and how simple', he thought.
>
> 'And the pain?' he asked himself. 'What has become of it?
> Well then, where are you, pain?' He turned his attention to it.
> 'Yes here it is. Well, what of it? Let it be.'

And death . . . Where is it?

He looked for his former accustomed fear of death and did not find it. 'Where is it? What death?' There was no fear, because there was no death.

In place of death, there was light. (*TSF*, p. 128)

In 1886, when Tolstoy was finishing *The Death of Ivan Ilyich*, he hurt his leg trying to help an old peasant woman, which led to a nearly lethal case of septicaemia. A long and painful recovery inspired the treatise *On Life*, in which Tolstoy supplemented his social and moral teachings with a general philosophy of life and death that brought together his belief in Nature and Reason, his interpretation of the Gospels and interest in Eastern religions and philosophy. The initial title of the essay was *On Life and Death*, but then Tolstoy cut the second noun, saying 'There is no death' (*SAT-DS*, I, p. 123).

According to this treatise, any individual existence is just a tiny particle of general life, and individual death is a necessary and liberating reunion with the whole. The only manifestation of general life available to humans is love, which can never be limited to one's kin and has nothing to do with the egotism and possessive instinct inherent in erotic infatuation, but unites the individual with humankind and thus with God. While universal love brings light and makes death blissful, sexual desire is akin to murder. In *Anna Karenina* Tolstoy compared Vronsky kissing Anna's body after their first lovemaking with a murderer striking an already dead victim with a knife.

The year after the publication of *The Death of Ivan Ilyich* Tolstoy started writing *The Kreutzer Sonata*, on which he worked until 1889. In that year he also wrote a draft of a story now known as *The Devil*. Both stories involved murders carried out or planned by men who were disappointed in their marriages. The basic facts behind each story came from real criminal cases, but Tolstoy processed them through his personal experience and imbued them with his own moral goals. Pozdnyshev, the main character of *The Kreutzer Sonata*, kills his wife out of jealousy; Irteniev in *The Devil* murders his former lover because, striving to keep his marriage chaste, he is unable to overcome his sexual obsession. In the first version of *The Kreutzer Sonata* Pozdnyshev was considering suicide as a possible outcome. As *The Devil* remained unpublished in Tolstoy's lifetime, the author did not have to choose between the two variants of the ending he drafted: in one alternative, instead of murdering his lover, Irteniev kills himself.

Tolstoy believed that the tragedies were caused by the sexual licence of young men before marriage, which had taught them to expect the same gratification of carnal desires from their family life. Irteniev's disaffection with his marriage finds its realization in the spell his former partner still holds over him; Pozdnyshev's manifests itself in hatred towards his wife and maniacal jealousy. Both male characters remain faithful to their wives, but the cost is insanity that drives them to murder or suicide. As he was writing *The Kreutzer Sonata*, Tolstoy told his daughter and his niece: 'There are no bad maidens, and there are no happy marriages.'

He was thinking, of course, of his own family history. The romance between Irteniev and a peasant woman, Stepanida, in *The Devil* strikingly resembles the relationship between Tolstoy and Aksinya Bazykina. In *The Kreutzer Sonata* the autobiographical context is less evident, but also present. Pozdnyshev's wife, after the delivery of her fifth child, submits herself to medical sterilization and starts looking to gratify her need for love. This finally draws her to adultery. Tolstoy's wife was considering the same type of contraceptive measures having given birth to her fifth child. In a way, Tolstoy was retrospectively imagining what could have happened had he not forbidden her to take such preventive actions.

Tolstoy's views on adultery were known to the reading public from his essays and not least from *Anna Karenina*. What made

The Kreutzer Sonata so shockingly new was the treatment of male romantic love depicted here as a socially acceptable manifestation of lust, a device for concealing the truth, most importantly from oneself. According to Tolstoy, society poeticizes romantic love and provides sentimental education for young people in order to make lust approvable and enjoyable for both sexes, teaching young females that their main duty is to be sexually attractive to males. In marriage, the nature of this social order becomes explicit; the oscillation of the Pozdnyshevs' relations between love and hatred reflects the rhythm of erotic passion.

Russian society was facing an irreversible process of female emancipation and ripe for the open discussion of sexuality. Tolstoy's views were militantly patriarchal, but he spoke about 'the cursed question' in his usual straightforward and unequivocal way. This opened the floodgates. The manuscript of the eighth draft of *The Kreutzer Sonata* had been given to the Kuzminskys. The text was lithographed and hectographed in hundreds of copies. When the censors banned publication of *The Kreutzer Sonata*, this only fuelled interest in the story, which was also published abroad and smuggled into Russia. Most readers were stunned by Tolstoy's analysis of the psychology of love, jealousy and murder, but were reluctant to subscribe to his moral conclusions. Some could not believe that the author could really have put his cherished thoughts in the mouth of a repentant murderer, and tried to reinterpret the text.

Many proponents of the 'soft' reading of *The Kreutzer Sonata* argue that in the final version, unlike the previous ones, Tolstoy deliberately leaves the reader in the dark as to whether adultery had actually taken place or whether it was the delusion of a jealous husband. For Tolstoy, however, feelings, motives and desires meant more than physical actions. He gave his story an epigraph from the Sermon on the Mount: 'But I tell you that anyone who looks at a woman lustfully has already committed adultery with her in his heart.' Pozdnyshev's wife 'committed adultery in her heart', and this was the only thing that really mattered for Tolstoy. To dispel all possible ambiguities, Tolstoy added an afterword in which he not only reiterated Pozdnyshev's views, but actually developed them further.

This approach was too extreme even for Chertkov, who by that time was happily married. The disciple pleaded with his teacher to provide 'half a page or just a few lines' showing that marital sex is permissible in 'a moral marriage'. He believed that Tolstoy's militancy would drive 'hundreds of millions of modern people' (CW, LXXXVII, p. 25) away from his teachings. Usually quick to accommodate his second alter ego, Tolstoy this time remained adamant. He responded to Chertkov's desperate plea with a clear statement that a moral marriage 'does not exist' (CW, LXXXVII, p. 24). He was aware that the way to moral perfection was full of obstacles and that he himself was not yet able to practise sexual abstinence within his family. From his perspective, it was possible to forgive human weakness, but not the obstinate refusal to see the truth, as he wrote around the same time to one of his followers: 'It is impossible to admit the slightest compromise over an idea' (Ls, II, p. 456).

In this particular case Sofia would probably have agreed with her arch-rival. In 1888 she gave birth to their last child, Ivan, who, as she sarcastically remarked, was the real 'afterword' to *The Kreutzer Sonata*. She wrote that the story humiliated her 'in the eyes of the entire world and destroyed the last love' in the family (SAT-ML, p. 167). At the same time, however, she went to St Petersburg for an audience with the emperor to ask him for permission to publish *The Kreutzer Sonata* in the edition of Tolstoy's collected works. Alexander III liked the story and Pobedonostsev found it useless to continue the ban against a work that was already widely circulating around Russia. The emperor granted the countess permission, but prohibited separate editions of the book, trying to keep it away from the attention of a mass audience: volume XIII with *The Kreutzer Sonata* appeared in three subsequent editions, the second of which was published in 20,000 copies.

There are numerous biographical, psychological and psychoanalytical interpretations of the roots of Tolstoy's attitude to sex. However, one cannot fully understand it outside of the general framework of his anarchistic worldview. Tolstoy saw sexual instinct as a coercive force. Unlike the state or the Church, this force was located inside the body, but that only made it more onerous, as it worked not through external repression, but through the manipulation of desires.

The ideal of chastity was not new to Russian culture and not limited to traditional monastic communities. In a much more radical way, a sect of self-castrators that had a widespread following among Russian peasants believed that men should get rid of the organs that lead them into temptation. Tolstoy firmly rejected this idea. The self-castrators were to him akin to revolutionaries ready to resist evil by violence. According to Tolstoy, an individual needed to free himself from the shackles of animal nature, not through a one-time act of enforced purification, but through incessant moral effort that was itself more valuable that any possible outcome. As he wrote to Yevgeny Popov, his collaborator at 'Intermediary':

If men were not lustful, there would be no chastity and no conception of it for him. The mistake is to set oneself the task of chastity (the outward state of chastity) and not the striving towards chastity, the inner recognition, at all times and in all circumstances of life, of the advantages of chastity over dissoluteness, the advantages of greater purity over lesser. This mistake is very important. For a man who has set himself the outward state of chastity as his task, a retreat from that outward state, a fall, destroys everything and halts a possibility of work and living. For a man who has set himself the task

of striving towards chastity, there is no fall, no halting of
his work; and temptations and a fall cannot halt his striving
towards chastity, but often actually intensify it. (*Ls*, II, p. 469)

Lust was the most powerful, but not the only, enemy with which
Tolstoy had to struggle. In order to let universal Christian love
reign supreme in his soul, he needed to overcome pride, vanity,
anger, bad feelings towards others, exclusive preference for his
kin, desire for physical comfort, fear of death and other inborn
passions. This was a lifetime task, an ideal he did not hope to attain
but merely to strive towards. In 1881 and 1884 he had resumed his
diary sporadically, but from 1888 onwards he kept it without major
interruptions until the end of his life in order to record all the
movements of his mind and to measure them against the gauge of
perfection he had created for himself.

The exhaustive struggle with his own bestiality and the egotism
that Tolstoy had envisaged for himself was seriously complicated by
the popularity of his teachings. When Tolstoy first became engaged
in theological research, Sofia had expressed her disappointment that
her husband was leaving the field that had brought him universal
fame for studies that could hardly have a dozen readers. It is difficult
to imagine a less accurate prediction. By the end of the 1880s Tolstoy's
fame has grown to outsize proportions.

The Holy Synod of the Russian Church banned Tolstoy's treatises,
but that did not prevent his ideas from reaching the widest possible
audience. In 1890 Pobedonostsev wrote to the emperor that it was
impossible

to conceal from oneself that in the last few years intellectual
stimulation under the influence of the work of Tolstoy has
greatly strengthened and threatens to spread perverted
notions about faith, the Church, government and society.
The direction is entirely negative, alien not only to the

Church, but to nationality. A kind of insanity that is
epidemic has taken possession of people's minds.[5]

Tolstoy's popularity was not confined to Russia. Converted and
potential followers were writing to him from all over the world
asking questions about the new revelation and seeking advice about
ways to live in accordance with it. Hardly any religious prophet ever
managed to gather such a flock within a decade from the day of his
first sermon.

Tolstoy owed the speed of his success to the very advance of
modernity that he loathed so much. Due to new cheaper printing
technology and standardized primary education, the works
published by 'Intermediary' could be sold in millions of copies.
Chertkov's managerial skills and English connections were also
instrumental in ensuring that Tolstoy's essays started to appear in
Europe at roughly the time his international fame as a novelist had
reached its zenith. Still, by far the most important factors were the
magic of Tolstoy's voice, the existential seriousness of his rhetoric,
his charisma and, no less importantly, perfect timing.

By the end of the 1880s Tolstoy had become the most famous
living novelist in the world. Both in Russia and outside of it, the
reputation of the author of *War and Peace* and *Anna Karenina* drew
the attention of the reading public towards his stance on religious,
moral and political questions. Moreover, the fact that Tolstoy was
revered among the rich and the powerful was, in itself, highly
significant for the masses that could not read long novels and
philosophical treatises. The peasants were more inclined to listen
to a repentant count than to 'one of their own'. The whole northern
hemisphere was in the throes of changes of incredible magnitude,
but nowhere else were the political system, social structures and
governing elites less able to cope with the challenge than in Russia.
The decisive moment for Tolstoy to test the appeal and limitations
of his teachings arrived in the second half of 1891.

By the summer of that year it had already become clear that a severe drought, following on from two poor harvests in 1889 and 1890, was leading Russia to face one of the most terrible famines of the nineteenth century. In August the government banned grain exports and belatedly started to take preventive measures. At the same time, public discussion of the approaching catastrophe was censored. This prohibition only increased panic. Nationwide the lack of grain was not that drastic, but the worst-hit regions were experiencing major shortages. Many peasants, who barely survived in the good years, were driven to extreme misery made worse by the epidemics that followed in the wake of the famine. The response to the disaster was bungled. Traditional distrust between central and local authorities and the government's suspicion of public philanthropic initiatives impeded successful cooperation.

Tolstoy was slow to get involved in the relief operation. He mistrusted philanthropy, believing money brought nothing but evil. When he realized the dimensions of the problem, however, he started acting with the fervour and efficiency of a true visionary. Soon he had become the centre of all private efforts. In spite of his aversion to questions of finance, he appealed to the Russian and global public for help and, capitalizing on the universal trust in his moral integrity, presided over the distribution of funds and regularly submitted reports to the press.

Within several months he had managed to collect more than a million roubles from different sources in Russia and abroad. Many donations came from the United States and Britain. Quakers were especially generous in both countries. This assistance helped him to organize and administer around 250 field kitchens providing free meals to 14,000 people. In addition to this, a further 120 kitchens were able to feed 3,000 children. Tolstoy not only coordinated these activities, but was constantly engaged in personally delivering necessary help to the needy. He also wrote a number of articles and essays raising public awareness of the

Tolstoy in 1891 in the village of Rusanovo taking part in hunger relief.

situation, breaking the official taboo against discussion of the famine. The government tried to ban these publications but was forced to react when they appeared abroad. When a Russian newspaper published Tolstoy's article 'The Terrible Question', accusing the authorities of hindering relief by not providing reliable information about regional supplies of grain, an official warning from the Minister of Internal Affairs was followed within a week by the launch of a statistical initiative to deal with the problem.

The famine brought Tolstoy's glory to its summit. Newspapers all over the world were writing about him, while in Russia the government, which believed that his articles 'must be considered tantamount to a most shocking revolutionary proclamation',[6] was unable to stop him. In Begichevka, the village that Tolstoy turned into his headquarters, the peasants were about to riot at the rumours, most likely false, that the police were planning to remove Tolstoy by force. The educated public was even more excited. Chekhov, not at all prone to elevated rhetoric, described him in one of his letters as 'a giant and a Jupiter' (Ch-Ls, IV, pp. 322–3).

These tragic events brought a temporary truce to Tolstoy's family. His adult children joined him in his efforts and worked in temporary kitchens in villages around the region. Sofia, who had to stay in Moscow with the younger ones, was assisting with financial transfers, record-keeping and correspondence with publishers. At last, she could sympathize with what her husband was doing and understand her own place in these activities. Tolstoy wrote in his diary on 19 December 1891, 'Joy. Relations with Sonya have never been so cordial. I thank Thee, Father, This is what I asked for' (Ds, p. 266), but unfortunately this idyll was not to last.

Predictably, Tolstoy himself was among the least satisfied with the results of his philanthropic work, describing his activities in Begichevka as 'stupid' in a letter to Strakhov, who was appalled (SAT-ML, II, p. 324). He knew those he managed to help were a tiny part of the several hundred thousand people who died during two years of hunger, along with the millions who barely survived. Moreover, he was aware that his efforts could not tackle the roots of the problem. The abundant harvest of 1893 did not mean that hunger, poverty and misery would end. He aspired to change the world and the soul of man, not merely to alleviate the consequences of hunger. In the midst of the relief operation, he was writing, rewriting and correcting his new book *The Kingdom of God Is Within Us*, in which he concentrated on the problem of non-violence, which he believed was the most important of the five commandments of Jesus.

Since Tolstoy first began to develop his particular Gospel, he found that he was not a voice calling in the wilderness. Many thinkers, sects and communes had been preaching and practising non-violence long before he was converted to the idea. Tolstoy sought to acknowledge the contribution of this disparate community of spiritual brothers and followers for whom he had become a natural leader. He set out to refute the objections of those who thought violence was compatible with Christianity or an engine of progress and necessary condition of human life. He would uproot an unjust and corrupt social order by attacking it at what he considered its most vulnerable point.

For Tolstoy, the power of rulers, government officials, generals and judges depended on the voluntary consent of millions of ordinary people to follow their orders. Thus the most effective way to undermine this was universal rejection of military service in any form. Tolstoy filled the pages of his book with the personal stories of people who had chosen to suffer persecution rather than take up arms or swear oaths that ran counter to their consciences.

Tolstoy had begun writing *The Kingdom of God Is Within Us* before the famine. On a train to Begichevka he had met soldiers sent to suppress riots caused by a dispute between peasants and a landowner over a mill. According to his follower and early biographer Pavel Biryukov, this encounter with decent, open-faced young men who were nonetheless ready to kill their brethren made as powerful an impression on Tolstoy as that of the death of his brother or the sight of the execution he had witnessed in Paris. In the conclusion to the book, Tolstoy explained this transformation of ordinary people into professional torturers and murderers as a kind of social hypocrisy that allowed a man to believe the atrocities he had to perform were necessary and justifiable. Tolstoy conceded that a person may not always be able to follow his conscience, but at least he should not deceive himself about the real motives for his behaviour. This sincerity was the first step on the road to moral regeneration. Anyone who let the 'Kingdom of God' enter his soul would finally find himself unable to resist it.

To submit such a work to a Russian publisher would have been pointless. Having finished the book in 1893, Tolstoy immediately sent it abroad both for translation and publication in the original. Rules were more lenient for books in foreign languages as their audience was inevitably limited to the educated classes, but in this case the Russian censors moved quickly to ban imports of even the French translation of 'the most harmful book they had ever forbidden' (cw, xxviii, p. 366). Nevertheless, this did not stop any literate Russian from reading it in hectographed copies.

Living according to the rules of the Kingdom of God was not easy. In September 1891, after prolonged conflicts, Tolstoy finally convinced his wife to publish a statement renouncing copyright for the works he had written after 1881, the year of his conversion. His earlier works, including the two great novels, remained Sofia's exclusive property. She also continued publishing and selling Tolstoy's collected works, even if their contents were not protected by copyright. The next spring Tolstoy gave his land away. Renouncing his rights as a landowner, he transferred ownership not to the peasants but to his wife and children.

This tortured compromise might possibly have worked as a divorce arrangement, but Tolstoy continued to live in the same house. He now had the dubious status of a dependant without responsibility for the well-being of his family and legally unable to interfere in any conflict that might arise between his family and the peasants. In his diaries, letters and conversations Tolstoy often expressed his revulsion at the 'luxurious' life he was living. Today's visitors to his houses at Yasnaya Polyana and in Moscow will struggle to notice this luxury. The houses seem modest, if not ascetic, and inadequate for such a large family. Tolstoy, however, compared himself not to his peers, but to the hungry peasants jammed in dirty huts. He found the minimal comfort he enjoyed unbearable, directly contradicting what he was preaching to a world that could observe and question the conflict between his teachings and his lifestyle.

Tolstoy's working room in Yasnaya Polyana.

The copyright agreement was no less precarious. In early 1895 Tolstoy promised his new story 'Master and Man' to Liubov' Gurevich, editor of the magazine *Severnyi vestnik* (Northern Messenger). In this story a rich merchant, Vasily Brekhunov, rushing to complete a profitable deal in spite of repeated warnings, orders his coachman Nikita to drive him in a snowstorm. They lose their way in the country at night. Suddenly, in an outburst of joy and tenderness he has never experienced before, Brekhunov unbuttons his fur coat and warms Nikita with his body, saving his life but dying himself instead.

Sofia had, by this time, reluctantly reconciled herself to the fact that her husband would publish his works for the benefit of the 'dark ones' in cheap editions from 'Intermediary'. But Tolstoy's preference for a highbrow literary magazine over her collected works edition insulted her. She concluded that his decision had been caused by an infatuation with 'the scheming half-Jewess' (*SAT-DS*, I, p. 233) Gurevich and went into a bout of jealous rage. Intending, or pretending to intend, to commit suicide, she rushed out of the house into the freezing night in her gown and slippers. Tolstoy caught her on the way and convinced her to return, but in the following days she made two new attempts to escape and was brought back by children. Later Sofia wrote that she had relished the thought of freezing herself to death like the character in Tolstoy's story. Finally, Leo backed down and agreed to let her publish the story simultaneously with *Northern Messenger*. Sofia recorded this in her diary on 21 February 1895. The same night their six-year-old son Ivan (Vanechka) fell ill. He died two days later.

Both Tolstoys knew that Vanechka was their last child and loved him with the tenderness and devotion of late parents. The boy himself was angelic: intelligent, kind, meek, totally devoid of childish egotism and endowed with a unique ability to understand others. As is typical in dysfunctional families, both parents were pulling their children in opposite directions: the daughters took Leo's side; the sons, with the exception of Sergei, the eldest, who tried to remain neutral and remote, sympathized with their mother. Vanechka was the only one who tried to bring the family together, showing unending love and compassion for both estranged spouses: 'Isn't it better to die than to see how people get angry?' he once said. The physical and moral suffering he experienced as a result of his parents' quarrels forced them to control their words and behaviour. In a way, he was the only remaining link that still united the family.

Shortly before his death, speaking to his mother about his late brother Alyosha (Alexei), Vanechka had asked whether it was true that children who died before they were seven became angels. Sofia told him that many people believed that. He replied, 'It would be better for me, Mama, if I too were to die before seven. My birthday will be soon. And if I don't die, dear Mama, let me fast so that I will not have sins' (SAT-DS, I, 512). After that he started to give away his toys and drawings as presents to his siblings and the servants.

'Mother is terrible in her grief. All her life was in him, she gave him all her love. Papa is the only one who can help her, but he suffers himself terribly and cries all the time,' wrote Tolstoy's daughter Maria in a letter to a friend.[7] Tolstoy, who believed that Vanechka would be 'his only son to continue the work of God after him' (SAT-DS, I, p. 515), had turned overnight from a strong and energetic middle-aged man into a sickly old one. He confessed to his wife that for the first time in his life he felt completely hopeless.

The young writer and future Nobel Prize laureate Ivan Bunin recalls how Tolstoy tried to overcome this despair. Bunin, who visited him in Moscow around that time, began telling Tolstoy how much he admired the recently published 'Master and Man':

[Tolstoy] turned red and waved his hands saying: 'Oh, let's not talk about this! It is a horrible thing; it is so worthless that I am

Sofia Tolstoy at the portrait of her late son Vanechka, 1895.

ashamed even to go out on the street.' On that evening his face was thin, dark and severe. His seven-year-old son Vanya had died only a short time before; so after disavowing 'Master and Man' he began to talk about his son. 'Yes, yes, he was a dear charming boy. But what does it mean that he is dead? There is no death.As long as we continue to love him, to live by him, he has not died.'

They went out into the snow. Tolstoy walked quickly, repeating abruptly, solemnly, harshly: 'There is no death, there is no death.'[8]

Tolstoy hoped that the love that Vanechka had brought to the world and common grief over this loss would recreate peace and understanding within the family. He wrote to Alexandra Tolstoy about his astonishment at the 'spiritual purity and particularly humility' with which Sofia had accepted the greatest loss of her life:

She . . . only asks Him to teach her how to live without a being in which she had invested the whole power of her love; and so far she does not know how to do so . . . None of us has ever felt as close to each other as we do now, and I have never felt either in Sonya or in myself such a need for love and such an aversion towards all disunity and evil. I have never loved Sonya as much as I do now. And I feel good because of it. (*Ls*, ii, p. 517)

His rigorous psychological analysis failed him here. The reconciliation achieved at the cost of a most terrible tragedy was short-lived. Leo was partially shielded by his philosophy, sense of mission and artistic genius. With none of these things to protect her, Sofia had to find refuges of her own. She had always passionately loved music and now found in it her only consolation. She would play the piano alone and with her husband and children, but her greatest joy came from performances by the famous pianist and composer Sergei Taneyev, Tchaikovsky's favourite pupil. After Vanechka's death, the Tolstoys invited Taneyev to spend the summer at Yasnaya Polyana. Like most Russian luminaries of the time, Taneyev admired Tolstoy and was happy to accept the invitation. Very soon members of the family could not fail to notice that Sofia's love for music was gradually transferring itself to the musician.

None of the participants in this triangle envisaged even the remote possibility of adultery. Taneyev, who was twelve years younger than Sofia, lonely and, most importantly, gay, enjoyed the attention of the great writer and the tender care of his wife. Once he realized, belatedly, that he had involuntarily provoked a family rift, Taneyev gradually distanced himself from the Tolstoys. Sofia was certain of the innocence of her behaviour and believed it was impossible to control one's inner feelings. Much later, she told her daughters that never in her life had she given so much as a handshake that she could not have given in the presence of her

Portrait of Sergei Taneyev, 1890s.

husband. Tolstoy was aware of this, but found Sofia's 'exclusive love' for another man humiliating, especially as it began during the period of their shared grief. Once he confessed that he was close to killing himself because of jealousy. He could not stop trying to convince Sofia that in order to get rid of an evil feeling, one must first admit that it is evil. At some point he confessed that he was on the verge of suicide from jealousy, shame and humiliation, but even that could not convince Sofia to renounce what she considered to be the only and totally innocent source of joy in her life.

In 1897, in the midst of this family crisis, Tolstoy finished his treatise *What Is Art?*, on which he had been working for the last ten years. Having addressed religion, philosophy, economy and politics, he now turned to a topic he knew intimately. Tolstoy challenged the identification of art with beauty prevalent in Romantic aesthetic thought. Instead, he claimed that art is a vehicle of human communication, a way of transmitting to others, and imbuing them with, the feelings of the author. While the artistic quality of a work depended on the sincerity and novelty of the emotions conveyed and clarity of their expression, its moral value was determined by the religious and ethical views of the author. Beethoven may have been a great musician, but the effect of his art on the souls of the Pozdnyshevs in *The Kreutzer Sonata* was detrimental and destructive.

Tolstoy attacked modern art not only on moral, but on artistic grounds. He quoted poems by Baudelaire, Verlaine or Maeterlinck that were, in his view, utterly incomprehensible. He understood that in the absence of universal criteria, this objection was relative – the same accusations could be made against the artists he himself admired. However, the notion of looking for a middle ground was not in his nature. Tolstoy had often denigrated his own work and did not hesitate to proclaim that, in order to be considered great, art should be understandable to everyone, including illiterate working people. He allowed for happy exceptions, but as a rule only folklore and religious parables could pass this threshold.

Did he fully believe what he was writing? In real life Tolstoy could not live without music. Taneyev was gradually replaced as his performer of choice by the young pianist Alexander Goldenveizer. In his memoirs Goldenveizer recalled a conversation in 1899 about a poem by Fedor Tyutchev, whom Tolstoy valued more highly than Pushkin and Fet:

L. N. told me: 'I always say that a work of art is either so good that there is no gauge to measure its value – this is true art. Otherwise, it is just all wrong. Look, I am happy that I found a true work of art. One I cannot read without tears. I learned it by heart. Wait, I'll recite it to you.' L. N. began with an unsteady voice: 'Blue-grey shadows mingled.' Even on my deathbed, I shall not forget the impression L. N. made on me then. He was lying on his back convulsively gripping in his fingers the edge of the blanket, trying in vain to contain his suffocating tears. Several times, he stopped and started again, but finally, when he reached the end of the first stanza, 'Everything is in me. I am in everything', his voice broke.[9]

Tyutchev's lyrical verse was a long way from being folk poetry, but came close to encapsulating Tolstoy's long-cherished idyll of a peaceful dissolution in universal love. Tears prevented him from reciting to Goldenveizer the final stanza of Tyutchev's poem: 'By the haze of self-oblivion/ Fill my feelings to overflowing/ Let me taste annihilation/ Mix me with the slumbering world.'[10] In spite of his denunciation of all modern artistic forms, at the time of his conversation with Goldenveizer Tolstoy was completing his third and the last major novel: *Resurrection*.

As usual, Tolstoy's work on the novel was long and tortuous. In 1887 he had been impressed by a story told to him by the lawyer Anatoly Koni about a man who, sitting as a member of a jury, suddenly recognized in the prostitute accused of theft a woman he had seduced many years earlier. Distraught and repentant, he decided to marry her, but the woman died from typhus acquired in prison before they could wed. At first Tolstoy insisted that Koni, himself a man of letters, should write about this case. Then, changing his mind, Tolstoy asked Koni if he could borrow the plot. Permission was readily granted.

It is not difficult to see why this story fascinated Tolstoy. Feeling perennial disgust towards himself and his former sexual exploits, Tolstoy was thinking about the psychological mechanics of repentance and the possibility of redemption. He believed that those who, like him, were unfit for abstinence should regard their first sexual encounter as a lifetime commitment. The hero of 'the Koni story', as Tolstoy always called it in his manuscripts, was not only ashamed of his role as seducer, but belatedly acknowledged that this seduction actually amounted to a marriage that needed only to be sealed.

Tolstoy strongly identified himself with the protagonist of the story. In 1903 he told Pavel Biryukov, who was writing his biography, that he had once seduced his aunt's maid, Gasha, who had subsequently perished after being driven out of the house. Five years earlier, however, writing in her diary about *Resurrection*, Sofia recalled that her husband had pointed out to her the same Gasha, now in her seventies and living in the house of Tolstoy's brother. Most likely we will never know whether Tolstoy's self-denunciation was caused by an erroneous memory or a deliberate desire to magnify his own guilt.

This time Tolstoy chose not to split his alter ego between two autobiographical characters. Instead, one gradually turns into another. Rich, prosperous and self-confident Prince Nekhlyudov, as he appears at the beginning of the novel, may be seen as a new incarnation of Prince Andrei or Vronsky, but then he is transformed into a sort of Bezukhov or Levin. After the reading of the first draft of the novel, Nikolai Strakhov suggested that Tolstoy was describing Chertkov's rebirth, an observation that seems especially pertinent if one remembers that Chertkov was for Tolstoy an idealized embodiment of his own spiritual quest.

The first draft of *Resurrection* was finished in mid-1895. It was a rather short story focused on the seduction and Nekhlyudov's repentance. It starts in the courtroom, where he sees Katyusha Maslova, the girl he had once seduced, accused of a murder she did not commit. The draft had a happy ending: the protagonist marries his newly rediscovered old love, emigrates to England and becomes a peasant in a commune. As all early versions of Tolstoy's major works, this draft was supposed to be revised and expanded, but Tolstoy could not bring himself to do this. He was distracted by his essays and reluctant to complete a work that could provoke conflicts of the kind he had experienced with 'Master and Man'. In 1897, however, he found a good reason to forge ahead.

The most radical of the many Russian sects receptive to Tolstoy's beliefs were the so-called Spirit Wrestlers, who rejected the institutionalized Church and had been exiled by Nicholas I to the Caucasus. In the 1890s one of their leaders was struck by the deep affinities between his beliefs and the ideas of the famous count and urged his followers to burn their weapons, denounce military service and refuse to take the oath of loyalty to Tsar Nicholas II. As a result of this, some Spirit Wrestlers were beaten to death, others were arrested or deprived of the means to survive in the severe mountain climate where they lived. Tolstoy and his associates issued an appeal on their behalf. Once again, Tolstoy himself was spared any repression, but other signatories, including Chertkov, were arrested. Because of his aristocratic connections, Chertkov was allowed to leave for England; two other prominent Tolstoyans were sent into exile.

Due to Tolstoy's intervention, the persecution of the Spirit Wrestlers began to attract international attention and the government felt compelled to grant them permission to emigrate to Canada. The resettlement of thousands of people was an expensive operation. Tolstoy therefore suspended, for a time at least, his resolve not to take money for his publications. He decided to donate the income from his new novel to help the sectarians. In the summer of 1898 he started reworking and expanding *Resurrection*.

Having found a valid excuse for writing prose, Tolstoy worked on it with intensity and passion. He turned the 'Koni story' into a full-scale novel that became the most elaborate artistic representation of his philosophy, and the broadest panorama of Russian life not only in his own fiction, but, arguably, in the whole of Russian literature. Apart from aristocrats, peasants and soldiers, whom Tolstoy always enjoyed writing about, the novel abounds with descriptions of civil servants, clerks, judges, gendarmes, merchants, clergymen, criminals and prostitutes. A significant part of the action takes place in Siberia, a place Tolstoy had never visited, but which had intrigued him since the time he had intended to write about the Decembrists. Nekhlyudov follows Katyusha there after her arrest and meets different sorts of convicts, including a number of revolutionaries.

Even before the novel was completed, the first instalments began appearing simultaneously in two versions: a censored one was published in the Russian magazine *Niva* (Field); the full one was printed in England through a press established by Chertkov. Complete editions appeared within weeks of the end of serialized publication and were immediately followed by English, French and German translations. Tolstoy's third novel reached a bigger audience in one year than his previous two had achieved in three decades.

On 28 August 1898, the day of his seventieth birthday, Sofia wrote in her diary that Leo 'was satisfied' as he had worked well on his novel:

'You know', he said to me when I entered his room, 'he won't marry her, I reached a final decision today and it is a good one!' 'Of course, he won't marry', I said, 'I told it to you long ago, if he were to marry, it would be false.' (*SAT-DS*, I, p. 405)

Sofia was also satisfied. Tolstoy's idea that a man should marry the first woman with whom he had carnal relations meant that she had, at best, no more reason to call herself his wife than Aksinya Bazykina, the housemaid Gasha and many other women, including the unknown prostitute in Kazan by whose bed the teenage Leo had wept in despair. Tolstoy, however, did not make Nekhlyudov change his mind. It is Katyusha who rejects him, preferring instead to marry a political prisoner. She loves the prince, but sacrifices her love because she does not believe he could be happy with her. At the end of the novel, Nekhlyudov reads the Gospels and discovers there the same five commandments of Christ that Tolstoy discussed in *What I Believe*. The final paragraph of the novel promises the dawn 'of new life' for its hero.

This ending and the whole story of a penitent intellectual and a good-hearted prostitute saving each other with mutual love and understanding was familiar to readers of Russian literature. In *Anna Karenina* Tolstoy had striven to rewrite *Madame Bovary*. In *Resurrection* he offered his own version of *Crime and Punishment*. In spite of his admiration for Dostoevsky as a person, Tolstoy disliked his narrative technique, 'monotonous language' and forced plots. He once noted, with surprise, that Dostoevsky, who had often fallen in love, could never describe love in a convincing way. He also agreed with Strakhov, who once said that Sonya in *Crime and Punishment* was implausible and found himself unable to believe in her.

The day he finished *Resurrection*, Tolstoy, in a familiar manner, remarked in his diary: 'It is not good. Not revised. Too hurried. But I am free of it and it does not interest me any more' (*Ds.*, p. 345). He continued, however, to be interested. The following year he expressed his intention to continue the novel. In July 1904 he wrote of his strong desire to write 'a second part of Nekhlyudov. His work, tiredness, nascent grand seigneurism, temptation by a woman, fall, mistakes and all against a background of the Robinson community' (*Ds*, p. 378). This urge to return to the finished and published text betrays dissatisfaction. Usually Tolstoy was in need of 'scaffolding' while writing, but having published the work he began denigrating it to be able to liberate himself and forge ahead. This time publication of the novel did not release him.

Chekhov described *Resurrection* as 'a remarkable work of art', but thought that the story lacked a real ending, and 'to write so much and then let everything be resolved with a text from the Gospels' was 'too theological'. He found the description of 'princes, generals, aunts, peasants, prisoners, guards . . . the most interesting', and the relations between Nekhlyudov and Katyusha 'the least interesting'. The majority of twentieth-century readers and critics have agreed with this assessment, with the exception of the universally admired seduction scene, the erotic power of which disgusted Sofia so much that she considered it inappropriate for their grown-up daughters.

In the same letter in which he discussed *Resurrection*, Chekhov expressed his attitude to the author:

> I am afraid of Tolstoy's death. If he were to die, there would be a big empty place in my life. To begin with, because I have never loved any man as much as him. I am not a believing man, but of all beliefs, I consider his the nearest and most akin to mine. Secondly, while Tolstoy is in literature, it is easy and pleasant to be a literary man; even recognizing that one has done nothing and never will do anything is not so dreadful, since Tolstoy will do enough for all of us. His work is the justification for the enthusiasms and expectations built up around literature. Thirdly, Tolstoy takes a firm stand, he has an immense authority, and so long as he is alive, bad taste in literature, vulgarity of every kind, insolent and lachrymose, all the bristling, exasperated vanities will remain in the far background, in the shade. Nothing but his moral authority is capable of maintaining a certain elevation in the so-called mood and tendencies of literature. (*Ch-Ls*, IX, pp. 29–31)

Chekhov died in 1904, six years before Tolstoy, and this letter was published in 1908. The elder writer, who had just turned eighty, was moved to tears: 'I never knew he loved me so much' (*Mak*, III, 39). He loved Chekhov as well, but could never establish with him any kind of kinship and suspected him of emotional coldness. In a similar way, Tolstoy believed that the artistic perfection of Chekhov's prose surpassed anything that previous writers, including Turgenev, Dostoevsky and himself, had been able to achieve, but he deplored Chekhov's lack of religious beliefs and serious moral purpose. There was, however, one exception.

'The Darling' is written with the laconic precision typical of the late Chekhov. Over a few pages he traces the entire life of a woman, Olga, who is first married to a theatre impresario, then to a timber merchant, after whose death she begins to cohabit with a vet who is separated from his wife and son. All her partners are described as hopelessly boring, but each time Olga is completely reborn, becoming first an ardent fan of the dramatic arts, then a respectable housewife with a deep understanding of the subtleties of the timber trade, and then a passionate animal lover. Finally she finds consolation in an attachment to the vet's son and becomes interested only in classical education and homework. Never in her life can she develop her own interests or opinions, borrowing instead from those she loves.

Tolstoy was not deaf to Chekhov's sarcastic detachment. He enjoyed reading the story aloud, laughing himself and making everyone around him laugh. Many memoirists recall that he was never successful in reading his own prose, but performed the works of the authors he loved brilliantly and that he especially enjoyed comic literature. However, whenever he read 'The Darling' to family members and friends he invariably ended up in tears. He had found in Chekhov's Olga the female ideal he longed for – a woman incapable of self-assertion who would willingly merge with him in one spiritual being. Later Tolstoy made a point of including the story whole in his *Cycle of Reading*, a personal commonplace book in which he tried to collect the best achievements of spiritual wisdom and moral beauty. In an afterword Tolstoy explained that, in his view, Chekhov had intended to condemn the 'Darling', Olga, but

a god of poetry forbade him to do it and ordered that
she be blessed, and he did bless her by involuntarily
covering that sympathetic creature in such a miraculous
light that it will forever remain an example of what a

woman may be to be happy herself, and make happy
those with whom fate had united her. (*CW*, XLI, p. 377)

For all he admired Chekhov's short stories, Tolstoy could never
reconcile himself to the plays, which, from Tolstoy's point of view,
lacked coherent plots and dramatic situations. Chekhov loved to
tell his friends that Tolstoy had once said to him: 'I cannot abide
Shakespeare, but your plays are even worse.' Worried that his
interlocutor was offended by his bluntness, Tolstoy took his hand,
looked into his eyes and said, 'Anton Pavlovich, you are a fine man,'
and then smiled and added, 'But your plays are still bad.'[11]

Chekhov believed that Tolstoy's frequent praise for his
contemporaries always carried a whiff of condescension and
Shakespeare was the only author whom he regarded as a worthy
rival. At least, Shakespeare was the only writer Tolstoy chose to
refute in a special essay that offered a devastating analysis of *King
Lear*, singling out psychological improbabilities, the incoherent
plot, bombastic language and the dubious morality of the tragedy.

Drama always fascinated Tolstoy, but it was only in 1886 that he
was able to make serious progress on a dramatic project. *The Power
of Darkness*, his first major play, shows that Tolstoy did not idealize
peasant life. The plot, based on an actual criminal case, included
adultery, murder, infanticide and the spectacular public repentance
of the murderer, which was vaguely reminiscent of *Crime and
Punishment*.

Alexander III initially approved the tragedy, but was later
convinced by Pobedonostsev to change his mind and ban stage
performances. *The Power of Darkness* was first performed in Paris,
followed by productions in nearly a dozen major European cities.
The first professional production of the play in Russia did not
take place until 1902, when Konstantin Stanislavsky directed and
played the main role at the Moscow Art Theatre. Eleven years
earlier Stanislavsky had already directed an amateur performance

of Tolstoy's comedy *The Fruits of Enlightenment*, which ridiculed the spiritualism that was fashionable in Russian society in the second half of the nineteenth century.

The two most important of Tolstoy's dramatic works did not appear on stage or in print during his lifetime. He started both in the 1890s, then put them aside to concentrate on *Resurrection*. He resumed work on them in 1900, probably influenced by the first production of Chekhov's *Uncle Vanya*, which he had seen that January at the Moscow Art Theatre. Tolstoy had left the theatre disappointed and certain that he could produce a more successful dramatic work of art. He nearly completed both dramas, but never tried to publish or stage either of them. *The Living Corpse*, the most theatrically successful of Tolstoy's plays, was published in the posthumous edition in 1911 and performed the same year at the Moscow Art Theatre, co-directed by Stanislavsky and Vladimir Nemirovich-Danchenko.

The main character of the play, Fyodor Protasov, ruins his family by squandering money on Gypsy singers. To free his wife and let her remarry a decent and loving suitor, he fakes his own suicide and disappears. This deceit is uncovered and both spouses are put on trial, Fyodor for fraud and his former wife Liza for bigamy. Eager to cut the knot that ties them both together and, no less importantly, understanding that the court's verdict will return him to his family, Fyodor actually kills himself.

Like *The Kreutzer Sonata*, *The Power of Darkness* and *Resurrection*, *The Living Corpse* was based on a real court case. Stories of crime and punishment fascinated Tolstoy no less than Dostoevsky, especially after the death of the latter. However, the plot of this play suspiciously resembled that of Chernyshevsky's *What Is to Be Done?*, in which one of the characters performs the same trick and is rewarded with complete success. Having always regarded divorce as being tantamount to adultery, Tolstoy found Chernyshevsky's novel deeply immoral. Nevertheless, Tolstoy's sympathy with Protasov's desire to free himself from family bonds is evident and Liza is portrayed as a kind and loving woman who is reasonably happy in her second marriage.

In his diary, Tolstoy referred to *The Living Corpse* as a 'small drama'. The moral conclusions of his 'big drama', *The Light Shines in the Darkness*, are even more controversial. This is the only major work by Tolstoy, in any genre, in which the main character is the conscious embodiment of his own religious and philosophical views. To the dismay of his family, Nikolai Saryntsev renounces military service, the Orthodox Church, landownership and money and tries to engage in manual labour. Most of the people around him regard his behaviour as madness, but the local priest, Vasily, and his daughter's fiancé, Prince Boris Cheremshanov, happen to be receptive to his teachings. The priest is evicted from the parish and forced to repent. Boris heroically refuses to renounce his views, rejects military service, is arrested and sent to a mental asylum and then a military prison. Lyuba, Saryntsev's daughter, despite her sincere love for Boris, agrees to marry another young man.

Tolstoy did not finish the play. From his plan, we know that in the final act Saryntsev was to be killed by Cheremshanov's mother, take the blame upon himself and die peacefully. However, the written text concludes with Saryntsev's desperate prayer: 'Vasily Nikanorovich has returned. I destroyed Boris. Lyuba is getting married. Am I wrong, wrong to believe in Thee? No. Father, help me' (*cw*, XXXI, p. 184). His spiritual anguish remains unresolved.

Dramatic form does not allow the author to claim omniscience. Tolstoy was deprived here of one of his main narrative tools – insight into the hidden depths of the human soul, revealing subtle motives and impulses that are unclear even to the person himself. Possibly these limitations, inherent in the genre, prevented Tolstoy from becoming a real rival to Shakespeare or Chekhov. At the same time, for the very same reason, Tolstoy could allow himself to be more intimate in his plays than in his prose, letters and even diaries, and to give voice to inner doubts for which he could not find an outlet elsewhere.

Saryntsev and Tolstoy suffered because of the contrast between their own safety and comfort and the plight of their followers. The government and the Church were keen to exploit this contrast by ignoring the leader and persecuting his flock. When some officials proposed to silence the dangerous writer, Alexander III adamantly refused, allegedly saying that he 'had no intention of making a martyr out of him and thus earning for myself universal indignation'.[12] Nicholas II, who inherited the throne in 1894, was not such a great admirer of Tolstoy's talent as his father, but continued the same policy. Protected by his fame, Tolstoy longed for the martyrdom of a real prophet and continued to provoke the authorities.

Tolstoy included in the text of *Resurrection* two passages describing a service in the prison church. The first was a merciless parody of the Eucharist. Tolstoy portrayed this ritual, familiar to every Christian, and a most sacred mystery of the Orthodox Church, as a weird and senseless piece of pagan magic. In the second passage he accused the Church of blasphemy and profanation of the letter and spirit of Christ's word. The real goal of established religions, Tolstoy suggested, was to switch off the personal conscience of believers, to allow them to continue their unjust ways of life and support a cruel and inhuman social order. Even submitting these fragments to the censors was unimaginable, but Chertkov, authorized by Tolstoy, included them in the foreign editions of the novel. Immediately thousands of copies of the full text appeared in Russia. Readers would hectograph the missing parts and stick them in the censored editions they bought.

Sofia, who was copying the manuscripts of *Resurrection*, wrote in her diary that she was 'disgusted by the intentional cynicism in the description of the Orthodox service' (*SAT-DS*, I, p. 444). For the official Church this was too much to stomach. After more than a year of discussion and deliberation, and, as recent historians argue, contrary to the will of Pobedonostsev, the Holy Synod issued an edict condemning Tolstoy in February 1901. The document was crafted with deliberate ambiguity. In its content it amounted to excommunication, but the word itself was not used. Instead the edict expressed sorrow that Tolstoy had severed his relations with the Church and hope that he would repent and return to its bosom. In any case, it was a consequential decision, making the writer an outlaw in his own country and, at the same time, enhancing his reputation especially among the younger generation that mostly detested the throne and the Church.

Tolstoy was unsure about the meaning of the edict. He asked his friends whether he had been officially anathematized, and looked disappointed having received a negative answer. In his reply to the Synod, he accused his opponents of hypocrisy and of inciting hatred and violence. He wrote that, walking in Moscow on the day of the publication of the edict, he had been called 'The Devil in human shape'. He chose not to mention the reaction of the crowd of several thousand people who, according to Sofia's diary, started shouting 'Hurray, L[ev].N[icolayevich]., hello L[ev].N[icolayevich]., glory to the great man! Hurray!' (*SAT-DS*, II, p. 15). As Chekhov wrote, 'the public reacted to the excommunication with laughter' (*Ch-Ls*, IX, p. 213).

In his letter to the Synod, Tolstoy confirmed that he had rejected the dogmas of the ruling Church and declared that repentance was impossible:

I must myself live my own life, and I must myself alone meet death (and that very soon), and therefore I cannot believe otherwise than as I – preparing to go to that God from whom I came – do believe . . . But I can no more return to that from which with such suffering I have escaped, than a flying bird can re-enter the eggshell from which it has emerged . . . I began by loving my Orthodox faith more than my peace, then I loved Christianity more than my Church, and now I love truth more than anything in the world. And up to now, truth, for me, corresponds with Christianity as I understand it. And I hold to this Christianity; and to the degree in which I hold to it, I live peacefully and happily, and peacefully and happily approach death. (CW, XXXIV, pp. 247, 252–3)

Tolstoy may have desecrated the sanctuaries of the official religion, but he had his own sense of what was holy and deserving of reverence. The moment of transition from an individual and temporal life to an eternal and universal one was for him sacred, as he wrote in his diary in 1894: 'Love is the essence of life, and death removing the cover lays the essence bare' (CW, LII, p. 119). His niece Elizaveta Obolenskaya recalled how he once asked the art critic Vasily Stasov about his thoughts on death. Stasov replied that he never thinks 'about that bitch'. According to Obolenskaya, Tolstoy took these words as blasphemy. She wrote that he often spoke about death as a 'blessing . . . a liberation, but thoughts about it worried him', and once he remarked that 'only frivolous people could not be afraid of death.'[13] It was not the fear of physical annihilation. Tolstoy was afraid he would not be able to prove himself worthy of this most solemn moment. At the end of his life, he confessed that while an unconscious death would be 'agreeable', he would prefer to die fully conscious.[14]

In the summer of 1901 Tolstoy fell gravely ill. The chief doctor of the Tula hospital where he was taken declared his state to be terminal. In the morning, when Sofia was putting a warm compress on his belly, he said, 'Thank you, Sonya. Don't think I am not grateful to you and don't love you.' Both wept. The next day, when he started feeling better he told her that he was at a crossroads: 'forward (to death) is good, and back (to life) is good. If I recover now it is only a delay.' After a pause, he added, 'I still have something that I want to say to people' (SAT-DS, II, pp. 22–3).

He recovered, but the doctors advised against staying in the damp and cold climate of mainland Russia. In late August the Tolstoys left for the town of Gaspra in the Crimean peninsula. Tolstoy there met with both Chekhov, who was living nearby in Yalta because of his worsening tuberculosis, and Maxim Gorky, the young revolutionary writer who had been exiled to the outer regions of Russia. Tolstoy took an interest in Gorky, eager to see in him a genius who had emerged from the Russian soil. Tolstoy's infatuation with his younger colleague proved to be short-lived and their ways parted irretrievably. In the autumn of 1901, however, the three most famous living Russian authors enjoyed their conversations and the chance to spend time together.

Chekhov and Tolstoy in Gaspra, *c.* 1901.

Gorky wrote in his memoirs that during their first meeting Tolstoy had called him the 'real man from the people'. He used the word *muzhik*, literally meaning a peasant, which was technically wrong. Like Chekhov, Gorky came from a family of tradesmen, but in his past he had led the life of a vagabond and enjoyed presenting himself as a social pariah. At the same time both Chekhov and Gorky shared a reverence for high culture that allowed them to overcome the limitations of their origins. Gorky, whom Tolstoy accused of being 'too bookish',[15] hated both his petit bourgeois background and the peasant culture to which his family was culturally close. He wrote later to Romain Rolland that he 'owed the best in him to books'.[16] Neither of the younger writers could sympathize with Tolstoy's desire to throw away the shackles of his elitist upbringing and imbibe the culture of the uneducated masses.

This literary idyll was arguably the last respite in Tolstoy's life. Shortly after the New Year he fell ill with pneumonia. On 27 January 1902 Chekhov wrote to his wife Olga Knipper-Chekhov, the famous actress of the Moscow Art Theatre, that news of Tolstoy's death would most likely reach her earlier than the letter he was writing. The next day Tolstoy's children and their spouses started arriving to bid farewell. Speaking to his sons, Leo said that he would die with the same faith with which he had lived for the last 25 years. He instructed them to ask him before his death, 'whether this faith was just',[17] and that he would 'nod in agreement' to let them know that this was of help to him in his last moments.

Against all expectations, Tolstoy's innate strength prevailed. A couple of months later he was again in bed on the verge of dying from typhus. Once again he recovered, but the illnesses had taken their toll, as Sofia recorded in her diary with a characteristic mixture of love and irritation: 'Poor thing, I can't look at him, this world celebrity, and in real life a thin, pathetic old man. And he keeps working writing his address to the workers' (*SAT-DS*, II, p. 69). Even after thirteen births and three miscarriages, she was still a

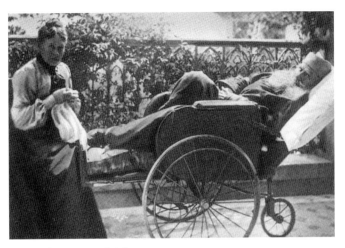

Tolstoy sick in Gaspra, with Sofia, *c.* 1902.

strong middle-aged woman. In the interval between her husband's two illnesses she managed to travel to Yasnaya Polyana and Moscow, taking in a visit to the opera and a private concert where Taneyev was playing. It was clear, at any rate, that the Crimea was not benefiting Tolstoy's health. In the summer of 1902 the couple headed home.

'How difficult are these transitions from dying to recovering,' Tolstoy said to Elizaveta Obolenskaya. 'I prepared myself for death so well, it was so calm and now I have again to think how to live.'[18] Tolstoy felt that he had lived his life to the end, but then was granted extra time. On his apparent deathbed in Gaspra he had prolonged conversations with his children and tried to gear his message to each of them. Likewise, he now set out to address his last words to different groups of the Russian population: the working people, the government, the clergy, the military and so on. He started this cycle with a letter to the emperor, whom he addressed as 'Dear Brother' and whom he urged to abolish private ownership of land.

The people who were close to him were departing. In 1903 Tolstoy wrote two farewell letters to Countess Alexandra Tolstoy, 'the Granny'. They both knew they would never be able to see each other again. A devout Orthodox Christian, she regarded her cousin's views as heretical. Their friendly relations continued, but both felt the barrier separating them. Leo made an effort to break it:

> The difference of religious convictions not only cannot and should not prevent the loving unity of people, but cannot and should not arouse the desire to convert a person you love to your faith. I write about [this], because I only recently understood it, understood that any sincerely religious person . . . needs his own faith that corresponds to his mind, knowledge, experience, and mainly his heart, and he cannot leave this faith. For me to desire that you would believe like me or for you that I would believe like you is the same as desiring that I would say that it is hot, when I feel cold or that am cold when I am burning with heat . . . Since then, I stopped desiring to bring others to my faith and felt that I love people, whatever their faith is. (*LNT & AAT*, p. 520)

Alexandra could not accept this olive branch. She was sure that there can be no salvation outside of the Church and in her last letter wrote that she prayed that God would finally grant 'the blessing of Holy Spirit' (*LNT & AAT*, p. 523) to her wayward cousin. She died in March 1904 at the age of 86. In August 1904 Tolstoy visited his dying brother Sergei for the last time. A convinced atheist, Sergei suddenly expressed his desire to receive communion. To the relief of Sergei's wife and their sister Maria, Leo fully supported this intention.

Both Alexandra and Sergei were his seniors and parting with them was to be expected. The most painful thing for Tolstoy was the loss of his daughter Maria (Masha), spiritually the closest to him among his children, the only one who refused to take her share when the estate was partitioned in 1892. 'Masha greatly alarms me. I love her very, very much' (*Ds*, p. 403), Tolstoy recorded in his diary on 23 November 1906. She died four days later with her father sitting at her deathbed. A month later, Tolstoy wrote:

> I go on living and often recall Masha's last minutes (I don't like calling her Masha, that simple name is so unsuitable for the creature who left me). She sits here surrounded by pillows and I hold her dear, thin hand and feel life departing, feel her departing. These quarter hours are among the most important, significant time of my life. (*Ds*, p. 404)

Vanechka's death eleven years earlier had brought the spouses together at least for a short while. This loss, however, only aggravated their growing alienation. Sofia did not want to conceal her belief that the hard physical work and vegetarianism imposed by her father had ruined Maria's health and made her unable to have children.

The house was emptying out. The only one of Tolstoy's offspring still living with her parents was their youngest daughter Alexandra. Highly intelligent and strong-willed, she was an ardent and rather rigid follower of Tolstoy's ideas. She adored her father, but was well aware that she could never be as intimately close to him as the kind and understanding Maria. In his delirium when he lay dying, Tolstoy would 'in a loud, joyous voice call out: "Masha, Masha!"' (*AT*, II, p. 404).

The only way to cope with these losses was to keep writing. Tolstoy always tried to balance a moral message with artistic perfection. In *The Forged Coupon*, an unfinished story about the contagiousness of good and evil, the former clearly prevailed, but in *Hadji Murat*, his other literary preoccupation of 1904 and the last major piece of prose he managed to bring near to completion, the opposite seems to be the case. Tolstoy was ashamed of his attachment to this story, but could not rid himself of the urge to perfect the work. In 1903 he wrote in his diary that his other plans were 'more important than the stupid Hadji Murat' (*Ds*, p. 370), but later confessed to his biographer Pavel Biryukov that he was still editing it during a visit to his sister, who lived in a convent. As Biryukov recalls, 'it was said in the manner of a schoolboy confessing to his friend that he had eaten a cake' (*CW*, XXXV, p. 629).

Hadji Murat was one of the most powerful chieftains in the Northern Caucusus and fought against the Russians in the wars of the 1840s and '50s. After quarrelling with Imam Shamil, the leader of the insurrection, he had deserted to the Russians but, finding out that they mistrusted him, tried to escape and was killed. The last part of this saga took place when Tolstoy was serving in the region. The character of Hadji Murat and his story had excited the young writer, who used to tell stories about him to his peasant pupils. Half a century later he brought his poetic imagination to bear on these old memories, supplementing them with new information from documents that had recently become available.

Tolstoy began writing the story in the 1890s but work intensified after his return from Gaspra. Although he was already a radical pacifist, in *Hadji Murat* he made no effort to conceal his fascination with the figure of a fierce and ruthless warrior. He began with an allegory of a thistle that survives in the field, retaining its wild beauty even under the plough, but which immediately loses its shape and flavour when torn from its native soil. Tolstoy initially planned to call his story *The Thistle*.

In 1904, as Tolstoy was working on *Hadji Murat*, a major new war had broken out in the Far East. For the first time in its history, Russia was fighting Japan, the new global power. Tolstoy's reaction was passionate and predictable. Once again, countries were being devastated and bankrupted. People were being separated from their families and everyday labours, taught to kill and dragged off to be killed or maimed for remote chunks of land that were equally useless to the populations of Russia and Japan. In the essay 'Bethink Yourself', Tolstoy protested not only at the mass institutionalized murder, but against the tribal ideology of patriotism that incited hatred towards other nations and races. According to his own profession of faith, the fifth commandment of Christ was never to view anyone as an enemy and not to divide people into tribes.

The horrific defeats suffered by the Russian army pained him nonetheless. His daughter Tatiana wrote in her memoirs that, having heard that Russian troops had abandoned the besieged Port Arthur, Tolstoy said that in his youth they did not surrender fortresses without blowing them up. When a Tolstoyan disciple present in the room, and 'apparently shocked by the Master's words', pointed out that this would lead to the loss of human lives, Tolstoy calmly responded: 'What do you expect? If you are a soldier, you have a job to do. And you do it properly.'[19] Deep inside him, there was still a warrior who could not brook surrender.

The situation was all too familiar to Tolstoy. As at the time of the Crimean War, in which he had fought as a young officer, the government tried to buttress a collapsing political order with a 'small and victorious war', as the Russian interior minister Vyacheslav von Plehve put it. Once again, the war turned out to be prolonged and bloody. Russia was defeated; von Plehve assassinated by a terrorist. Revolution broke out in 1905.

Like Hadji Murat, who could not find his place among the rebels or with the Russians, Tolstoy could not align himself with either side in the growing divide that was tearing Russian society apart. In 1906 Tolstoy published his 'Address to the Russian People', in which he predicted that the government that tried to combine half-hearted political concessions and promises of constitutional reform with new waves of repression would not be able to withstand the revolution 'under its banner of autocracy even with constitutional amendments'. It could save itself 'not by a parliament elected in whichever way and even less so by guns, cannon and executions, but only by admitting its sin before the people and trying to redeem itself' (CW, XXXVI, p. 304).

For the first time Tolstoy attacked the revolutionaries even more fiercely than the authorities. He accused them of being ready 'to blow up, destroy and kill' (CW, XXXVI, p. 306) out of a belief in some abstract form of social order, about which they could not even agree among themselves. According to Tolstoy, the government and the opposition shared the same contempt for ordinary people, trying to impose upon them their own views and prejudices. He urged millions of Russian peasants not to resort to violence, but to stop obeying orders and laws.

In August and October 1905 a terrified emperor issued decrees abolishing censorship, guaranteeing basic civil freedoms and announcing the formation of the State Duma, Russia's first national parliament, which did not, however, receive the right to appoint the government. Belated and forced concessions only increased agitation and militancy. Tolstoy did not believe in political reforms. His main concern was the situation in rural areas, where peasants were burning down the houses of landowners and demanding redistribution of the land. As a rule these uprisings were controlled and contained by the leaders of the peasant communes. Given the dimensions of the turmoil, the level of physical violence remained relatively low.

Tolstoy saw the revolutionary crisis as a make-or-break moment that would either bring peace to Russia and consequently to the whole world, or end in a nightmare of bloodshed and destruction. He believed he knew how to adjust the social order in a way that would pacify the country. Age and precarious health notwithstanding, Tolstoy was tireless in propagating the socio-economic theories of a thinker who had influenced him no less than Rousseau or Schopenhauer.

The American progressive economist Henry George was one of the most popular social theorists of the second half of the nineteenth century. His philosophy brought together socialist and libertarian ideas in a synthesis that Tolstoy found especially appealing. Like many intellectuals of the time, George had tried to identify the causes for the stark contrast between rapid technological progress and growing poverty.

George's most famous book, *Progress and Poverty*, was published in 1879 and sold several million copies. George supported the notion of private property insofar as it concerned the products of a person's own labour, but not for natural resources: land, in particular, he considered an indivisible asset of humanity. At the same time, he did not propose the nationalization of land. Instead, he suggested the 'nationalization of rent' from it in the form of a universal land tax, the level of which would depend upon the productivity and location of the land. In *Progress and Poverty* George tried to demonstrate by meticulous calculations that a correctly calibrated land tax would increase the productivity of land, lead to its redistribution in a way favourable to farmers, provide enough income to abolish all other taxes and sustain a modest social security network.

It is unlikely that Tolstoy checked George's figures, but he referred to them as a theorem that had been proven beyond reasonable doubt. He even proposed a range of tax rates that, he believed, would allow Russia to keep the land profitable for cultivation and avoid speculation. He found in George a system that struck him as being fair, simple, reasonable and, most importantly, congruent with the natural sense of justice prevalent among the peasants. In George's economic theories he had found a 'green stick' that would eventually bring happiness to humanity.

Unlike George, Tolstoy was an anarchist who rejected, as a matter of principle, not only the notion of taxation, but the very idea of the state itself. Nonetheless, the ideas of the American theorist showed him a possible way to peacefully transform the current order into a world in which people willing to engage in agricultural labour would have access to enough land and others would have to produce the goods and services necessary for those who cultivate the land. In this utopian world, states, governments and laws would themselves become redundant.

Tolstoy had discovered Henry George in February 1885, when he wrote to Chertkov that he 'was sick for a week but consumed by George's latest [*Social Problems*] and the first book *Progress and Poverty*, which produced a strong and joyous impression' on him:

> This book is wonderful, but it is beyond value, for it destroys all the cobwebs of Spencer–Mill political economy – it is like the pounding of water and acutely summons people to a moral consciousness of the cause and even defines the cause . . . I see in him a brother, one of those who according to the teachings of the Books of the Apostles [has more] love [for people] than for his own soul. (*cw*, LXXXV, p. 144)

Moved and flattered by Tolstoy's approval, Henry George wanted to come to Russia to talk to the great man, but his health did not permit him to make such a journey. When George died in 1897, Tolstoy wrote to Sofia that he was shocked by the death and felt as if he had lost 'a very close friend'. Around the same time, he made Nekhlyudov in *Resurrection* give away his land according to George's principles: 'What a head this Zhorzha was' (*cw*, XXXII, p. 231), an old peasant says admiringly, having finally understood the plan. Tolstoy's interest in Henry George reached its peak during the revolution of 1905, when he wrote a foreword to the translation of *Social Problems* that had been made by his follower Sergei Nikolaev and several essays popularizing Georgism.

In June 1907 Nicholas II dissolved the Duma and issued a new electoral law ensuring the victory of loyalists at the next elections.

This gave de facto dictatorial powers to Pyotr Stolypin, the minister of interior affairs he had appointed a year before at the height of revolutionary upheaval. Stolypin was known for personal courage, fierce independence and had the reputation of a reformer. Stolypin was also Tolstoy's distant relative; Tolstoy had personally known and liked his father.

The Russian public hated Stolypin, but this did not deter Tolstoy from acting. In July 1907 he wrote a letter to the all-powerful minister pleading with him to pay attention to *Social Problems*. As Stolypin did not reply, in October Tolstoy wrote again, asking Stolypin to help an old Tolstoyan who had been arrested and reproaching him for ignoring his first letter. This time the minister answered. He promised to reconsider the criminal case, but not his policy and ideas. He gave a nod to the theories of George, but insisted that these could only be applied in Russia in the remote future:

Do not think that I did not pay attention to your letter. I could not answer, because it wounded me too much. You consider evil what I believe to be good for Russia. It seems to me that the lack of landed property is the cause of all our problems. Nature has imbued man with some inborn instincts like hunger, sexual feelings, and one of the most powerful feelings of this order is the sense of property. One cannot love what belongs to another as well as that which is one's own and a man will not take care of land he uses on a temporary basis in the same way he would take care of it were it his own . . . I have always considered you a great man, and I have a modest opinion of myself. I have been lifted up by the wave of events, most likely just for a moment! Still, I want to use this moment to the utmost extent of my strength, understanding and feelings for the benefit of the people and my motherland, which I love as they used to love it in the old time. How then can I possibly do what I do not think and consider to be good? And you write to me that I am following the way of evil deeds, ill fame, and most importantly – sin. Believe me, that feeling often the possibility of an approaching death one cannot help thinking about these questions, and my way seems to me to be the honest one.[20]

Stolypin's goal was to undermine the peasant commune, the institution most cherished by Tolstoy. Stolypin hoped to put in the place of these communes millions of private landowners who would transform Russian agriculture and the national psyche. In order to provide the land necessary to establish these future American-style farmers without a major land redistribution programme, Stolypin envisaged a mass voluntary resettlement of peasants to Siberia. The Trans-Siberian Railway, which had started functioning in the first years of the century, provided the necessary logistical means to fulfil this plan.

Stolypin had already survived several assassination attempts. Tolstoy could therefore appreciate the power and seriousness of his correspondent's convictions, but was not able to accept his views. He regarded exclusive preference for one's own to the common and universal in the same way that he regarded sexual instincts, that is, as something to be fought against, not condoned and cherished. To turn the resources given to humans by God into private property was, for Tolstoy, tantamount to 'contemporary slavery' or another kind of serfdom. Moreover, the concept of private land property was, according to him, antithetical to the very essence of the Russian peasant soul. Stolypin's plans looked to Tolstoy like a new incarnation of Peter's Westernizing reforms that could only be imposed in the same way, by violence and coercion.

In October 1907 Tolstoy again wrote to Stolypin, using as a pretext the arrest of one of his assistants. With the letter, he sent a copy of Social Problems. In January, not having received an answer, he again pleaded with the minister to think of his own soul and start doing things that corresponded to the hopes and aspirations of the majority of Russians:

> You who have already suffered so cruelly from attempts on your life, who are considered to be the most powerful and energetic enemy of revolution, you would suddenly take the side not of revolution, but of eternally distorted truth, thus eliminating the soil that breeds revolution. It might well happen that, however softly and cautiously you would act in suggesting such a new measure to the government, they may not agree with you and remove you from power. As I can understand you, you would not be afraid of this, because you do, what you do now, not to keep yourself in power, but because you consider it to be just and necessary. Let them remove you 20 times, slander you in all possible ways, this would still be better than your current situation. (*CW*, LXXIX, p. 43)

This letter was signed, 'loving you Lev Tolstoy'. Stolypin again agreed to intervene in the case Tolstoy mentioned, but had nothing more to say in response. Both were growing tired of each other. Tolstoy later said that it was childish of him to believe that the government would listen to him, but he was still glad he had written to the emperor and to Stolypin, at least to be sure that he had done 'everything to find out that it is useless to address them'.[21] Still he felt himself responsible for being so forgiving towards a person he increasingly regarded as a serial murderer or, as he wrote in his last unsent letter to Stolypin in August 1909, 'the most pitiable man in Russia.' (*Ls*, II, p. 690)

To implement his reforms, Stolypin needed to suppress the revolution and he was doing this with increasing cruelty. He started by introducing courts martial for civil crimes. Executions, extremely rare in Russia for a century and a half, were taking place on a daily basis and on an unprecedented scale. Each day the now liberated press reported on new hangings and shootings. On 9 May 1908, after reading one such report, Tolstoy began recording his article 'I Can't Be Silent' on a phonograph, but he was overpowered by emotion and soon found himself unable to continue. He spent the whole following month carefully working on the text, which became what is arguably the most famous and most powerful denunciation of capital punishment ever written in any language. Extracts from it appeared on 4 July 1908 in several Russian newspapers, all of which were fined for publishing it.

Tolstoy begins the article with a naturalistic, detached description of a hanging in which his indignation manifested itself only in the precision of his account of the horrifying details. He wrote about the situation in the country, where hatred was growing and little children were now playing out terrorist acts, expropriations and executions in their games. He insisted that, while all killing is abominable, soldiers who obey orders, terrorists who risk their lives, and even actual executioners, who are mostly illiterate and know that their job is disreputable, are more deserving of pardon than the cold-blooded and self-righteous murderers who send people to the gallows. In closing, Tolstoy acknowledged his own moral responsibility for everything that was happening in his country:

Everything now being done in Russia is done in the name of the general welfare, in the name of the protection and tranquillity of the people of Russia. And if this is so, then it is also done for me, since I live in Russia . . . And being conscious of this, I can no longer endure it, but must free myself from this intolerable position! It is impossible to live so! I, at any rate, cannot and will not live so. That is why I write this and will circulate it by all means in my power, both in Russia and abroad. I hope that one of two things may happen: either that these inhuman deeds may be stopped, or that my connection with them may be terminated by my imprisonment, whereby I may be clearly conscious that these horrors are not committed on my behalf. Or better still (so good that I dare not even dream of such happiness), I hope that they put on me, as on those twelve or twenty peasants, a shroud and a cap and push me too off a bench, so that by my own weight I may tighten the well-soaped noose round my old throat. (*CW*, XXXVII, p. 94–5)

The resonance of the article was comparable only to that of Zola's *J'accuse*, published ten years earlier. Tolstoy was accustomed to admiration and hatred. He had already received death threats and remained unfazed. Still, he was aware that whatever he wrote, he would not be arrested or hanged. For twenty years, the tragedy he described in *The Light Shines in the Darkness* had been torturing him.

In his later years Tolstoy was especially friendly with Maria Schmidt, an old spinster who had adopted his philosophy and settled near Yasnaya Polyana, sustaining herself with hard manual labour. She was so humble and kind that even Sofia, who disliked Tolstoyans, always mentioned her favourably. Schmidt did not approve of 'I Can't Be Silent' because it lacked 'love'. With enormous difficulty, she managed to convince the author to omit personal attacks on Stolypin, Nicholas II and others. Tolstoy, who called hatred 'the most painful of all feelings', was struggling to contain his fury. Worst of all, it was a fury born of despair.

Overcoming strong resistance from the left and the right, Stolypin succeeded in bulldozing his main reforms through the Duma. The peasants were granted the legal right to leave the commune while retaining their strips of land as private property that they could farm or sell, to buy state land and receive subsidies for resettlement. The peasant commune was doomed. Stolypin wrote that twenty years of internal and external peace would transform Russia – this dream proved to be no less utopian than Tolstoy's Georgism. He was assassinated by a terrorist in 1911 just as he was about to be dismissed from his post. With the revolution

Maria Schmidt: the exemplary Tolstoyan, 1886.

suppressed, the emperor no longer needed a ruthless reforming zealot at the helm of the government. Three years later, Russia entered the First World War, which ended in a new revolution, followed by civil war and later the annihilation of the Russian peasantry in the horrors of forced collectivization and the Gulag. Tolstoy was fortunate not to witness these developments, but he could read the writing on the wall.

In the summer of 1908, when Tolstoy was writing 'I Can't Be Silent', Chertkov returned to Russia after being amnestied, and settled nearby. Conversations with his old friend and favourite disciple gave a lot of comfort and support to the ageing writer. Staying at Chertkov's house, Tolstoy used to wander around and talk to peasants without being recognized. At Yasnaya Polyana, where everyone knew him, this would have been impossible. He recorded the growing plight and hardening resentment of the poor, who started speaking about the educated elite as 'parasites', an epithet Tolstoy had never heard before. Use of this word did not bode well for the privileged; later it became a Bolshevik catchword that justified the extermination of the ruling classes. Some conversations, however, were different.

During one of his strolls, Tolstoy met a handsome, intelligent and hard-working young peasant who quickly acquiesced to the stranger's admonitions about alcohol and promised to quit drinking. Tolstoy could hardly believe in such rapid success, but that evening the young peasant came by to borrow brochures about the evils of intoxication. With obvious satisfaction, he conveyed his mother's gratitude to the old man. Proud of himself, he also confessed that he was already engaged to a nice girl.

Having congratulated the convert, Tolstoy asked a question 'that always interested him when he dealt with the young nice people of our time':

Forgive me for asking, but please, tell the truth,
either don't answer or tell the whole truth.
   He looked at me calmly and attentively. 'Why is not to say?'
Have you sinned with a woman?
   Without a moment's hesitation, he answered simply,
'God save me, this has never happened.'
   That is good, really good, I said. I am glad for you.

Tolstoy published an essay about this conversation under the
title 'From the Diary'. Several days later, he added a conclusion and
a new title, 'Grateful Soil'. The full text appeared in late July 1910:

What a wonderful soil to sow, what a receptive soil. What
a terrible sin it is to throw there the seeds of lies, violence,
drunkenness, debauchery . . . We, who have a chance to give
back to this people at least a bit of what we have ceaselessly
been taking from them, what do we give him in return?
Aeroplanes, dreadnoughts, 30-storey buildings, gramophones,
the cinematograph and all the useless stupidities that we call
science and art. And most importantly, the example of empty,
immoral, criminal life . . . 'Woe unto the world because of
offences! for it must needs be that offences come; but woe to
that man by whom the offence cometh!' (cw, xxxviii, pp. 35–6)

This turned out to be the last work he published in his lifetime.
   Tolstoy was never a stubborn technophobe. He rode a bicycle,
recorded his voice on a phonograph sent to him by Thomas Edison,
used trains and put photographs on the walls of his room. He often
said that there was nothing inherently good or bad about railways:
the main problem was where and for what reason does one travel.
Modernity in his eyes failed this litmus test. There was no hope for
the peasant he encountered, even if the young man would be able to
abstain from drinking and remain chaste. For decades, Tolstoy was

Tolstoy in 1908.

fighting against the overwhelming force of history. He had never surrendered, but now he knew that it was time for him to leave the battlefield.

4

A Fugitive Celebrity

Since the time he suddenly left university at the age of eighteen, Tolstoy's life had been full of forced breaks and abrupt departures. He resigned from the army, stopped teaching at his school and gave up managing his estate. He rejected the dissolute life he had led in his youth and then the respectable lifestyle of a rich landowner. He abandoned the Orthodox Church and the social class into which he had been born. He also made several attempts to break up with literature, but each time he had returned to writing.

In October 1864 Tolstoy fell from his horse and broke his arm while hunting. After an unsuccessful intervention by local doctors, the bone started to heal in the wrong way and it became clear that a new operation would be necessary. This was performed in Moscow at the house of his father-in-law, who made sure to engage the best surgeons in the country. According to the memoirs of Tatiana Kuzminskaya, having received the first dose of anaesthetic, Tolstoy 'jumped up from the armchair with wide-open staring eyes, threw away the sachet of chloroform and shouted loudly: "My friends, one can't live like this . . . I think . . . I have decided . . ."' (*Kuz*, p. 315). He was given another dose, calmed down and the operation went successfully.

Whatever Tolstoy had 'decided' in his delirium, the urge to liberate himself from something he cherished always lived inside him. The stronger the bonds were, the more desperate he was to break them, however painful it was – particularly if it was painful.

There was nothing in the world he valued more than family. In spite of or because of this, even during the happiest periods of his life he could not rid himself of a yearning to escape. In the early 1880s, when he renounced the Church, money, property, authorship, meat, tobacco, alcohol, hunting and so on, these thoughts became obsessive. 'He cried today loudly that his most passionate thought was to leave the family,' wrote Sofia in her diary on 26 August 1882. 'Even on my deathbed I will not forget the sincerity of his exclamation; it was as if my heart had been cut from inside me' (SAT-DS, I, p. 108).

Tolstoy was experiencing an almost physiological need to leave behind his 'position as a famous writer' and a comfortable life and to join the thousands of homeless wanderers who lived off nothing more than the fruits of their daily labour and alms. One of his younger disciples once asked him where a true follower of Tolstoy's religion was supposed to dine. 'Don't be worried,' came the mentor's answer, 'whoever needs you, will feed you.'[1] He was unable to perceive Sofia's attitude towards him as love, and he wrote in his diary on 5 May 1884: 'Dreamed that my wife loved me. How simple and clear everything became! Nothing like that in real life. And that's what is ruining my life . . . It would be good to die' (Ds, p. 186).

Several weeks later, after an argument with Sofia, who had accused him of financial recklessness, he packed his bag and left home. He 'wanted to leave for good', but her advanced pregnancy made him 'turn back halfway to Tula'. The next morning their last daughter, Alexandra, was born. His urge to leave did not recede. Late in 1885 Sofia wrote to her sister Tatiana that Leo had told her he wanted to divorce her and go to Paris or America, as 'he can't bear to live like this.' By the end of the row that followed, according to Sofia, Leo was sobbing hysterically: 'Can you imagine, Levochka shaking and twitching from sobs' (SAT-ML, I, pp. 499–500).

Twelve years later, in the midst of the family crisis over Sofia's infatuation with Taneyev, Tolstoy wrote her a farewell letter:

> Dear Sonya,
> I have been long tormented by the incongruity between my
> heart and my beliefs. I have not been able to make you change
> your life or your habits, to which I have myself accustomed you
> and up to now I haven't been able to leave you . . . Neither was
> I able to continue living any longer the way I have been living
> for the last sixteen years, now struggling and irritating you;
> now yielding to the temptations to which I was accustomed
> and by which I was surrounded, and I have now decided to do
> what I have long wished to do – to go away. (*Ls*, II, p. 561)

Tolstoy did not deliver this letter and did not leave either. He
believed the Gospels compelled him to leave his family and
everyone he held dear in order to follow his calling, but he was also
convinced that universal love could manifest itself only through
love to those who are close by. It was, after all, a sudden feeling of
compassion towards his wife and son that had allowed Ivan Ilyich
to renounce his animal egotism and die peacefully.

Tolstoy's enemies and followers alike accused him of hypocrisy.
He was pained by these reproaches, but able to withstand them
because he knew them to be false. The pleasures derived from
everyday comforts would never be able to influence his decisions.
He was less sure about the temptations of lust and earthly fame.
His struggle with both of these is evident in *Father Sergius*, a piece
in which the intensity of contained passion is breathtaking even
by the standards of Tolstoy's prose. Tolstoy spent most of the
1890s devising and writing this story before it was completed in
1898. It was never published in his lifetime. The story starts with a
description of the sensational disappearance of a highly successful
person:

> In Petersburg in the eighteen-forties a surprising event occurred.
> An officer of the Cuirassier Life Guards, a handsome prince

who everyone predicted would become aide-de-camp to
Emperor Nicholas I and have a brilliant career, left the service,
broke off his engagement to a beautiful maid of honour, a
favourite of the Empress's, gave his small estate to his sister
and retired to a monastery to become a monk. (*TSF*, p. 235)

Prince Stepan Kasatsky changes his life so dramatically because
his bride confesses to him that, before their engagement, she had
been a mistress of the emperor. This discovery turns Kasatsky's love
into a sham and exposes the futility of his ambitious aspirations.
Religious beliefs he has preserved from his childhood save him
and guide him to a monastery where he takes holy orders as Father
Sergius. From there he retires to a remote cell where he leads an
ascetic life of prayer and abstinence. His solitude is, however,
marred by recurrent doubts about his choice and by carnal
desires. In one of his worst moments he is tempted by an eccentric
aristocratic beauty, who comes to his cell specially intending to
seduce the handsome hermit. Father Sergius manages to resist the
temptation only by cutting off one of his fingers.

This incident, which soon becomes public knowledge, makes
the recluse immensely popular and gives rise to rumours about his
healing powers.

> More and more people flocked to him and less and less
> time was left him for prayer and for renewing his spiritual
> strength . . . He knew he would hear nothing new from
> these folk, that they would arouse no religious emotion in
> him, but he liked to see the crowd to which his blessing
> and advice was necessary and precious, so while that crowd
> oppressed him, it also pleased him. (*TSF*, pp. 256–7)

Tolstoy was thinking of himself, his newly acquired status as a
prophet and of the crowds of people who came to seek his advice.

His son remembers that, after the departure of a particularly annoying guest, Leo would start jumping wildly through the rooms of his house followed by a line of hilarious children. They used to call this silent ritual of liberation 'Numidian cavalry'. His daughter Tatiana once asked him about a strangely clad man in his room. 'He is a young member of what's to me the world's most strange and incomprehensible sect,' responded her father, 'the tolstoyans.'[2]

In May 1893 he noted in his diary that 'as soon as a person is able to free himself a little from the sin of lust, he immediately stumbles and falls into the worse pit of human fame'. Thus it was necessary not 'to destroy existing bad reputation, but to value it as a means to avoid the greatest temptation . . . I need to elaborate on this topic in "Father Sergius". It is worth it' (*CW*, LII, p. 82).

The limits of Father Sergius's pretended saintliness are laid bare by a plump, imbecilic and sexually voracious merchant's daughter, who makes him succumb to the desires of the flesh. The world of the hermit and his faith are ruined. 'As usual at moments of despair, he felt a need of prayer. But there was no one to pray to. There was no God' (*TSF*, p. 263). Tolstoy initially planned to make the hermit kill the girl, but that would have made the story a second version of his earlier novella, *The Devil*. Instead Tolstoy transformed the story of sex and murder into one of escape. In a trademark paradox, ugly sin liberates Father Sergius from the slavery of earthly fame and enables him to serve God by serving people. The hermit leaves his cell and is saved from utter destitution by a hapless old childhood friend, who lives a life of self-sacrifice supporting her desperate daughter, sickly and useless son-in-law and two grandchildren, without ever thinking that she is doing anything good or moral. Father Sergius becomes a wandering beggar, is arrested and exiled to Siberia. There he settles down, working in the kitchen garden of a well-to-do peasant, teaching his children and attending to the sick.

This ending seems to have been borrowed from another escape story Tolstoy considered writing in the 1890s. *Posthumous Notes of the Elder Fyodor Kuzmich* were based on a popular legend about Alexander I, according to which the emperor, known as a mystic and visionary, did not die in 1825, as had been officially announced, but escaped and lived under the assumed name of Fyodor Kuzmich. Fyodor was a real person. Like Father Sergius, he had wandered around Russia and been arrested for vagrancy and exiled. In his old age he lived in Siberia working in the kitchen garden of a merchant and teaching peasant children in return for meals – the old man never took money. Fyodor died in 1864, leaving behind some encoded papers. His identity was never revealed.

Tolstoy was inclined to believe the legend, but he did not write the story. He had too many other commitments in the 1890s to be able to bury himself in the documents and achieve the historical accuracy and sense of truthfulness he required. The themes of sudden escape, downturn in lifestyle, arrest and manual labour in a Siberian kitchen garden were transferred to *Father Sergius*. In 1901 the Russian historian Nikolai Schilder published a four-volume comprehensive biography of Alexander I. Schilder did not fully subscribe to the tale of the emperor's escape, but also he did not refute it and seemed to be cautiously sympathetic to the legend. The biography, with its wealth of material, gave a boost to Tolstoy's design. In 1902 he met Grand Duke Nikolai Mikhailovich, also a court historian, in Gaspra and talked with him about his relative. According to the grand duke, Tolstoy thought that if Alexander 'really ended his life as a hermit, his redemption would be complete' (*cw*, XXXVI, p. 585). In the writer's mind such a transformation would redeem Alexander from the sin of having been complicit in the murder of his father, and the no less horrendous crime of ruling over other human beings for nearly a quarter of a century.

In 1905 Tolstoy started drafting the story narrated as an autobiography by the eponymous Fyodor Kuzmich. He had made

Tolstoy at work, drawing by Ilya Repin, 1891.

little progress by 1907 when Grand Duke Nikolai Mikhailovich published a monograph disproving the legend beyond reasonable doubt. It was likely, he concluded, that Fyodor was a fugitive nobleman, but definitely not the emperor. Thanking the grand duke for the book, Tolstoy wrote:

> Let the impossibility of identifying Alexander and Kuzmich as the same person be proven historically, the legend still remains alive in all its beauty and truthfulness. I started writing about it; but shall probably not go on. No time, I have to pack for the forthcoming transition. It is a pity. What a charming image. (*cw*, LXXVII, p. 185)

He was charmed by the sudden and mysterious disappearance of a tsar and could not stop dreaming about it. In the midst of the revolutionary turmoil, Tolstoy felt an almost regal sense of mission

Tolstoy, 28 August 1903.

weighing down upon him and the responsibility this entailed. These provoked, in turn, an irresistible urge to escape. He could not yet allow himself to withdraw from the public stage, but he had all but withdrawn from the world of literature.

Since the publication of *Resurrection* he had almost stopped publishing original artistic works. When the first posthumous edition of his complete works appeared in 1911, the reading public was stunned by *Father Sergius, Hadji Murat, The Living Corpse* and many other hidden treasures. The impact was similar to that achieved earlier with the publication of his great novels. 'Tolstoy's Alyosha the Pot. Never read anything greater,'[3] wrote the leading Russian Modernist poet Alexander Blok about a four-page story about the life, love and death of a hard-working and selfless village boy considered a fool by some, for his kindness and readiness to oblige others.

There were many reasons for Tolstoy's reluctance to publish. He wanted to avoid family rows about copyright; he also felt compelled to mortify his authorial vanity. Still he was physically unable to stop writing fiction. In 1909 he was working on a big story that was tellingly entitled *There Are No Guilty People in the World*. He confessed in his diary that he still had 'an urge to do artistic work, not real desire of the kind I had before with a clear goal, but without any goal or rather with a hidden and unattainable goal of peering into the human soul. And I want it very much' (*cw*, LVII, p. 52). On 2 October 1910, a month before his death, he had a new creative idea and exclaimed, 'What a great thing that could be!' (*cw*, LVIII, pp. 110–11).

Tolstoy needed to build himself 'a scaffolding' to write, but at the same time he was consciously trying to turn his literary pursuits into an innocent eccentric pastime for an old man, like playing cards for no money, horseriding or listening to Mozart on the gramophone. When rumours began to spread that he was about to be awarded the Nobel Prize, he wrote a letter to one of his Swedish friends asking him to plead with the Academy to avoid

Tolstoy on horseback at the age of eighty, 1909.

'putting him in the very unpleasant position of refusing it' (*Ls*, II, p. 660). He did his best to prevent major celebrations for his eightieth birthday in 1908.

His main literary preoccupation at that time, however, was to find a form of self-effacement not only in the world of publishers and readers, but within the text itself. For several years he had been working on *A Cycle of Readings*. The purpose of this commonplace book of quotes and selected passages was to serve the needs of labouring people who did not have enough leisure time to spare on books. Arranged as a calendar, it collated quotations from major religious and moral teachers of all ages and nations from Lao Tzu and Confucius to Tolstoy himself. These were the fruits of Tolstoy's years of digging through piles of books searching for pearls of wisdom that were both profound and digestible. He even found a valuable thought in Nietzsche, a philosopher he detested. Daily entries were accompanied by longer 'weekly readings' designed for

Sundays and consisting of short stories and essays. For this purpose Tolstoy edited folk stories, religious parables and the works of dozens of writers including Turgenev, Maupassant, Anatole France and others. Some he inevitably wrote himself. The longest of these was his story *The Divine and the Human*, in which he set out to demonstrate the vanity and futility of revolutionary activity.

In *A Cycle of Readings* Tolstoy tried to dissolve his own input in an ocean of universal wisdom and morality to become just one voice in a great chorus. His creative role may have been confined to the choice and arrangement of material, but he was still shaping the artistic mainstream of the epoch. His role was akin to that of a theatre director or an orchestral conductor, two professions that were then acquiring their own independent artistic value.

Having completed *A Cycle of Readings*, Tolstoy started compiling *For Every Day*, later published in English as *A Calendar of Wisdom or Wise Thoughts for Every Day*, a work of the same sort addressed to even less educated readers. Here weekly readings were replaced by daily ones, simplified and rearranged in thematic order. This led to another compilation called *The Way of Life*, which abandoned the calendar altogether and arranged the texts thematically. This book, published in small instalments, dealt with the most pressing questions of religion, morality, life and death, sin and virtue. Tolstoy continued editing it until his death. He now included more of his own texts, presented in a short aphoristic form almost entirely devoid of the characteristic features of his authorial voice. *The Way of Life* was arguably the most personal of Tolstoy's books in terms of its existential meaning, and the most impersonal in terms of style. He was trying to escape from his own expressive power to let unadulterated truth speak for itself.

In the meantime, Tolstoy's marriage turned from dysfunctional to outright miserable. During the 1905 revolution his wife and sons had summoned police to arrest peasants cutting wood in their forests, and called armed guards to protect the estate. Having legally transferred ownership of the land to the members of his family, Tolstoy could do nothing to stop this but the peasants, the press and the Tolstoyans accused him of hiding behind his wife's back. So did Sofia herself.

Chertkov's return to Russia had given Tolstoy an opportunity to resume conversations with a friend he had greatly missed and brought relief from the unbearable atmosphere at home. However, Chertkov's presence strongly aggravated the crisis in his family. Sofia considered him the cause of all her troubles and did not hold back in her diary: 'A scoundrel and despot. He has taken the poor old man in his dirty hands and makes him perform evil deeds' (*SAT-DS*, II, p. 212). She compared Chertkov to the Devil, playing on the etymology of his surname, derived from *chert* ('the devil') (*SAT-DS*, II, p. 213). Sofia also spread rumours about the homoerotic nature of her husband's attachment to Chertkov.

There were two basic reasons for the quarrels. One was Tolstoy's diaries. Tolstoy had himself encouraged Sofia to read them many years before, but he changed his mind after the utopian ideal of merging his own being with that of his wife collapsed. In the cramped confines of the house at Yasnaya Polyana, however, there were few opportunities to hide the papers. He started to keep secret diaries for himself alone, hiding them under the upholstery of the armchairs. He passed some manuscripts to Chertkov, but backed down after this provoked a series of rows with Sofia. It is to Sofia's credit, however, that after her husband's death, when she had the diaries at her full disposal, she crossed out only five words, three of which scholars are still unable to read.

Copyright was an even more divisive issue. Tolstoy's decision to transfer his works to the public domain was legally valid only until his death; after that the rights would automatically revert to Sofia as his legal heir. Some of his sons threatened to start legal proceedings against him to invalidate his decisions on the basis that he was suffering from a mental disability. Given Tolstoy's precarious status as a quasi-excommunicate outlaw, this was not a hollow threat. On the other side, Chertkov was pressing the old man to settle the question of copyright once and for all. Finally Tolstoy gave in and drew up a will, certified by a lawyer, in which he bequeathed the beneficial rights to all his works to his daughter Alexandra, a passionate Tolstoyan and Chertkov's most trusted friend in the family. Chertkov was appointed as his literary executor. Unable to face the tumult this would cause with Sofia and other members of his family, Tolstoy signed the document secretly in the forest.

His reasons for doing this were self-evident and justifiable. Chertkov's devotion, competence and efficiency had been tested many times. Tolstoy's will was also beneficial for future generations of readers and scholars. Under the Bolshevik regime, Chertkov, protected by official reverence towards his mentor, managed to launch an academic edition of Tolstoy's complete works and to organize a team of researchers able to sustain and complete this ninety-volume *chef-d'oeuvre* of academic publishing after his death in 1936.

Nevertheless, on a personal level, Tolstoy's decision violated at least three important tenets of his self-professed faith. He had signed a legal document, authorizing the state, with its laws, courts and executive powers, to intervene in his family affairs. He had done this secretly, making it necessary for Alexandra to lie to her mother. Tolstoy had also always argued against thinking about the future, which is beyond our control, and advised focusing one's moral duty on the present. His favourite slogan was, 'Do whatever you must, come what may.' Now he had failed to apply this precept.

Neither Leo nor Alexandra was any good at dissembling. When confronted by Sofia's direct questions, they both had to resort to hopeless ambiguities. As Tolstoy had always predicted, the truth came out, justifying Sofia's suspicions and accusations. From her point of view, by conspiring with Chertkov behind her back he had proved himself to be hypocritical, secretive and scheming.

She threatened to murder Chertkov and – repeatedly – to commit suicide. She was reading her husband's diaries and believed he was doing the same with hers. As a consequence, mentions of suicide in her diaries were often accompanied by assertions that she actually possessed the means to kill herself.

Tolstoy tried to pacify her with concessions on issues that were not existentially important for his soul. In 1909, contrary to his usual aversion to giving public speeches, he agreed to go to the peace congress in Sweden, possibly looking for an excuse to get away from home. Sofia, frightened that he would not come back, started to object vehemently and, after several clashes, he backed down. In the summer of 1910 she managed to extract from him a promise to stop seeing Chertkov. Suspicious that he would break his word during one of his walks, she spied on him from a cave in the forest. Leo's strategy was self-defeating. Sofia interpreted his concessions as a sign that she could achieve more by pressing harder. Tolstoy knew this, but confessed that the moments when he gave in brought him pure and unadulterated joy, while standing firm, or worse, allowing himself to react angrily, made him suffer and feel ashamed of himself.

On 26 September 1910, after a furious quarrel with her mother, Alexandra left and went to stay with Chertkov, swearing never to return home. A week later, on 3 October, Tolstoy suddenly fainted and experienced a total loss of memory when he came round. When he had partially recovered, Sofia asked Alexandra to forgive her and released her husband from his vow not to see Chertkov. Alexandra relented but told her mother that, had Tolstoy died from this fit, all the world would have blamed her for it. Clearly this was the only kind of argument capable of carrying any weight with Sofia.

Some members of the family, including Tolstoy himself, believed Sofia was insane. In July 1910 the leading Russian psychiatrist Grigory Rossolimo concluded that she was showing symptoms of hysteria and paranoia, and predicted that the couple would not be able to go on living together. Others suspected her of feigning madness in order to manipulate her husband and pointed to her full recovery after Leo's death. This interpretation seems unlikely even if there was method in her madness.

In one of her diary entries, Sofia recorded that she had inadvertently knocked Leo's portrait off her table with her notebook, adding, 'In the same way I am throwing him from his pedestal with this diary' (SAT-DS, I, p. 400). This task was beyond her power and, in reality, she never tried to accomplish it. She needed her own place on the pedestal, and was ready to fight for it with all the means at her disposal. Tolstoy wrote on 15 September 1910, 'Not to mention her love for me, of which not a trace remains, she does not need my love for her either, she only needs one thing: for people to think that I love her. And it's this that is so dreadful' (Ds, p. 464). His worldview did not allow him to see that Sofia's aspiration to preserve for posterity her role as the wife of a genius was the only thing that made her life meaningful to her after her children had grown up. Leo had stopped loving her 'exclusively' and her ideal love for Taneyev had evaporated.

By now Sofia's main and possibly only preoccupation was to archive her own version of her life story. A particular bone of contention was photographs. On 21 October 1910, after looking at a newspaper photograph of herself and Leo, she wrote: 'Let more than a hundred thousand people see us together holding each other's hand as we have lived all our lives' (SAT-DS, II, p. 222). After threatening suicide, running away from home, scandals and quarrels, she wanted others to believe in her happy family life. These stage-managed displays of family harmony were especially painful for Leo, who wrote with disgust about Sofia's desire to be photographed as a happy couple. She objected to his photographs with Tolstoyans and made him take Chertkov's photograph off the wall. When Leo was reproached for doing this by Alexandra and put the photograph back, Sofia tore it down again and burned it.

Last photo of Lev and Sofia as a happy couple, on the 48th anniversary of their wedding.

Sofia's identity was restored after Tolstoy's death. Now no one could challenge her status as a widow. She even finally accepted de facto the distribution of roles established in Tolstoy's will. While Chertkov assumed responsibility for publishing, she took upon herself the position of guardian angel of the Yasnaya Polyana and Moscow houses. She managed to preserve both from the horrors of revolution and civil war.

It is no wonder, therefore, that Sofia was so preoccupied with Leo's diaries and that she was especially sensitive to the way in which these represented his love for her. She once read an entry in which Lev expressed his retrospective inability to understand his own reasons for marrying: 'I was never even in love, but I could not help getting married' (*Ds*, p. 476). In reply she pointed out extracts from his earlier diaries in which, in his own words, he spoke of his passionate love. He had nothing to say. He just could not remember his feelings, as Pierre Bezukhov was unable to imagine himself being made happy by the death of his wife when talking with Natasha. Like Pierre, Tolstoy had changed beyond self-recognition.

After a sudden loss of consciousness in 1908, Tolstoy's memory, which used to be impeccable, began to fail him. Of the things that happened to him during the last years of his life, few gave him such unmitigated pleasure: finally his mind was freeing him from its enslavement to his past. Tolstoy believed that history was retained in the present and thus could be understood and reconstructed by retrospective analysis. Documents were either redundant or, at best, could only play an auxiliary role in this process. Likewise, an individual, at any given moment of his life, was just an embodiment of his experience in its entirety. There was no need to remember specific episodes:

If I were to live in the past, or at least be conscious of and remember the past, I would not be able to live a timeless life in the present as I do now. How then is it possible not to rejoice in the loss of memory. Everything I had worked for in the past, for example the inner work expressed in my writings, is in me to live by and to use, and I cannot recall the work itself. Amazing. And I think that this joyous change happens to all old people: all your life concentrates in the present. How nice! (*cw*, LVIII, p. 121)

What marked the life he was now living was tension between the desire to escape and an acute consciousness of his duty to stay. In July 1910 he started keeping a diary 'for himself only', which he tried to hide from Sofia. 'I am bearing up and will bear up as much as I can, and pity and love her. God help me' (*Ds*, p. 477), he wrote on 8 September. Tolstoy reproached himself for unkind feelings towards his wife, reminding himself two weeks later that 'The main thing is to remain silent and remember that she has a soul – that God is in her' (*Ds*, p. 478). On 25 October he confessed to a 'sinful desire on my part that she should give me an excuse to go away. That's how bad I am. I think of going away and then I think of her situation, and I feel sorry and I can't do it' (*Ds*, p. 483).

The same day he spoke about his intention to leave with Alexandra. On the next day, he sought advice from Maria Schmidt, one of the very few Tolstoyans who understood the reasons he chose to stay in the family and who was friendly with Sofia. Schmidt was appalled. 'It is a weakness, it will pass,' she allegedly told him. 'It is weakness', replied Tolstoy, 'but it won't pass.'[4] The next day, as Tolstoy recorded, 'nothing special happened. Only my feeling of shame increased, and the need to take some step.' On the evening of 28 October, already far away from Yasnaya Polyana, he wrote one of the most frequently quoted diary entries in literary annals:

Went to bed at 11.20. Slept until after two. Woke up, and again as on previous nights, I heard the opening of doors and footsteps . . . It was Sofia Andreyevna looking for something and probably reading. The day before she was asking and insisting that I should not lock my door. Both her doors were open, so that she could hear my slightest movement. Day and night, all my movements and words have to be known to her and to be under her control. There were footsteps again, the door opened carefully and she walked through the room. I don't know why, but this aroused indignation and uncontrollable revulsion in me. I wanted to go back to sleep, but couldn't. I tossed about for an hour or so, lit a candle and sat up. Sofia Andreyevna opened the door and came in asking about 'my health' and expressing surprise at the light, which she had seen in my room. My indignation and revulsion grew. I gasped for breath, counted my pulse: 97. I couldn't go on lying there and suddenly I took the final decision to leave. (*Ds*, pp. 469–70)

Shortly before his marriage, gendarmes had raided his estate searching for clandestine publications. Nearly half a century later, his own wife was raiding his working table and his bedroom looking for papers she thought he was concealing from her. Tolstoy woke up Alexandra, her friend Varvara Feokritova and his doctor Dushan Makovitsky, who helped him to pack. Having written a farewell letter to Sofia, he left the house before six o'clock, accompanied by Makovitsky and leaving Alexandra behind to deal with the inevitable consequences.

Dr Makovitsky had been living at Yasnaya Polyana for the past six years. After Tolstoy's illnesses in Gaspra, Sofia had insisted on having an in-house medic. Although he was not fond of doctors, Tolstoy agreed to this because Makovitsky was an ardent Tolstoyan. His professional abilities may have been questionable, but his love and devotion to his patron were not. From the time of his arrival until Tolstoy's death, Makovitsky performed the role of a Russian Eckermann or Boswell, carefully documenting every sentence pronounced by his host.

To run away, however, was not enough. A fugitive must go somewhere. Tolstoy's favourite characters just disappeared, but this solution worked only in fiction. Heading to a railway station, Tolstoy asked Makovitsky where he could go to be 'further away' from home (*Mak*, IV, p. 398). Makovitsky suggested Bessarabia, where they could stay with a Tolstoyan they both knew and liked, and then try to get abroad. Tolstoy was considering other options. He wanted to see his sister Maria, the only person he knew and loved from childhood who was still alive.

Maria Tolstoy was two years younger than Lev. Throughout their lives the two youngest children had been especially close. After a disastrous marriage and a stormy separation, Maria lived abroad for several years with a Swedish viscount, Hector de Kleen, and had a daughter with him. Afterwards she deeply repented her illicit love and became fervently religious. In 1891 she entered a convent at Shamordino, near the famous monastery of Optina Pustyn', which Tolstoy had once frequently visited.

In spite of their diverging beliefs, the siblings loved each other. In April 1907, telling her about his grief over the loss of his daughter and her namesake Maria, Lev wrote to his sister:

> I often think about you with great tenderness, and in the last days, it is as if some voice keeps telling me about you, how I would wish, how it would be nice to see you, to know about you, have contact with you . . . I am your brother both in blood and in spirit, do not reject me. (*CW*, LXXVII, p. 77)

'Dear friend Levochka, my dear brother in blood and spirit,' Maria answered. 'How touched I was by your letter. I wept reading it and am now writing touched to the depths of my heart' (*CW*, LXXVII, p. 78).

Tolstoy arrived at Optina late in the evening of 28 October and stayed the night at the monastery inn. The next morning Chertkov's assistant, Alexei Sergeenko, to whom Tolstoy had sent a telegram about his whereabouts from the railway station, brought distressing news from Yasnaya Polyana. Having heard about Leo's escape, Sofia had run to drown herself in the pond, slipped on the bridge and fallen into the shallows. Carried home by Alexandra and Tolstoy's secretary, Valentin Bulgakov, she had oscillated between an intention to repeat her suicide attempt and the urge to bring her fugitive husband home. Sofia kept saying that if she were to get him back, she would sleep on the floor in the doorway of his bedroom so as not to allow him to escape again.

Tolstoy dictated his last article against the death penalty to Sergeenko and walked around the grounds of the monastery, thinking about the possibility of remaining there. He longed for an environment that would allow him to 'pack for transition', as he had put it several years before. He hoped that the walls of Optina Pustyn' might protect him from tactless curiosity, alien intrusions and the struggle with himself, but he was not contemplating the possibility of rejoining the Church. Later he told his sister that he would gladly obey the rules that applied to novices, if only he were to be allowed not to attend services and not cross himself.

This solution was impracticable. The authorities at the monastery could hardly accept an unrepentant heretic, excommunicated by the Synod, who was, on top of everything else, legally married. Tolstoy could not fail to envisage the problems he would face and decided against visiting the monastery's elder. In the afternoon he left Optina for Shamordino. 'Is it bad at home?', asked Maria, seeing the state in which her brother had arrived. 'It is terrible,' Leo answered and started crying.[5]

At Shamordino he spent the last enjoyable evening of his life with his sister and her daughter Elizaveta Obolenskaya, whom he had always loved:

Mashenka made a very comforting and joyful impression on me . . . and so did dear Lizanka. They both understand my situation and sympathize with it. On the journey I kept thinking as I was travelling about a way out of my situation and hers, and could not think of any, but there surely will be one, whether we want it or not, and it won't be the one we foresee. Yes, I should only think about not sinning. And what will be, will be. (*Ds*, p. 471)

By then he had all but decided to settle in Shamordino near his sister. Also that evening Alexandra arrived with fresh news and letters from the family. Sofia pleaded with him to come back or at least to allow her to see him, promising to renounce luxury, follow his way of life and reconcile with Chertkov. In the morning Tolstoy went to rent a hut and made an arrangement with a peasant widow, but then changed his mind, scared that Sofia would catch up with him.

In the afternoon the whole group sat over a map choosing a place to go: Bulgaria, the Crimea and the Caucasus were suggested. Tolstoy was hesitant about the direction, but adamant that he was not going to a Tolstoyan commune because he wanted to live in an ordinary peasant hut. Leadership was one of the things he had renounced; he imagined for himself a kitchen garden, like the one where Father Sergius or Fyodor Kuzmich had found their last abode. He went to bed without making up his mind, but in the night he panicked and once again woke up Makovitsky and Alexandra.

On 31 October they caught the first morning train and bought tickets to the southern city of Rostov-on-Don. There they would be able to choose their next destination. Tolstoy wrote letters to his sister, apologizing for his sudden departure, and to Chertkov, informing him that he was probably going to the Caucasus. By the middle of the day, however, he became seriously ill. Very soon his companions saw that he was unable to travel and had to get off the train at Astapovo station. The station did not have an inn, but the stationmaster, who happened to be a Tolstoyan himself, offered them the two best rooms in his house. The last letter he started to dictate was addressed to his English translator, Aylmer Maude, on 3 November: 'On my way to the place where I wished to be alone I was taken ill' (*Ls*, II, p. 717); he was too weak to continue.

To be alone was his only wish. In a telegram sent from Astapovo to Chertkov he said that he was 'afraid of publicity', but publicity was inevitable. News about his escape appeared in the newspapers the morning he left Shamordino; in the train he was recognized by other passengers, who rushed to his coach to satisfy their curiosity. Within a day the little railway station became the main provider of breaking news to the whole world from Japan to Argentina. Reporters, photographers, cameramen, government officials, police agents, admirers and gawpers started swarming to Astapovo. Tolstoy's flight brought him further into the limelight. Trying to evade the advance of modernity, he had contributed to its triumph by creating one of the first global media events.

Wanting to return to nature, he ordered that his body be buried in an unmarked grave near the place where as a child he had searched for the mythical green stick. His wish was granted, but his grave became a major global tourist attraction. The absence of a name plaque eloquently shows that none was necessary. Who needs a plaque on the Holy Sepulchre?

Arguably Tolstoy was not able to imagine the scale of the sensation he had caused, but he had some idea of what was happening. During the first days of his stay at Astapovo, he asked for the newspapers to be read to him, leaving out news about himself. The attention he received was burdensome for him; after one medical intervention he exclaimed, 'And the peasants, the peasants, how they die'. The day before he died he reproached those around him for 'concerning themselves with Lev alone', when 'there are a great many people in the world besides Lev Tolstoy' (*AT*, II, pp. 404–5).

Tolstoy's grave in
Yasnaya Polyana.

The selected pool of visitors allowed to approach his bedside also kept growing. Chertkov arrived on 2 November, calm, confident and decisive as usual. Goldenveizer and Tolstoy's publisher, Ivan Gorbunov-Posadov, arrived the next day. Tolstoy criticized Goldenveizer for having cancelled a concert: 'Peasants do not leave the field even if their father is dying, and the concert is your field.'[6] He told Gorbunov-Posadov that he was unable to look at the proofs of the new instalments of *The Way of Life* he had brought to Astapovo.

Sofia and the children, with the exception of Sergei, who had arrived earlier, came on 4 November and stayed in the specially chartered railway carriage that had brought them. Sofia, however, was not allowed to see her dying husband. The unanimous view of Tolstoy's followers and his children was that such a meeting would be fatal for him. Sofia wandered around the outside of the stationmaster's house, peeping through the window and giving interviews to journalists about her 48 years of happy family life. Her every step was recorded, photographed and filmed. She was summoned to give Lev a final kiss and to ask him for final forgiveness only a few hours before his death, when he was unconscious or already seemed to be.

Did Tolstoy understand or suspect that Sofia was close by as he was dying? Since his departure he had been thinking and inquiring about her, and expressing his love and pity for her. At the same time he wanted to avoid meeting her at all costs, at least during the first days of his illness when he was still hoping to recover and continue his journey. He had been on the brink of death many times and got used to it. Only on 4 November did he hesitantly say, 'It seems I am dying. And, may be, not.' Did he change his mind when the prospect of eternal separation became imminent? At one point in his last days, when he was already half-delirious, he said to his eldest daughter Tatiana: 'So many things are falling on Sonya. We managed things badly.' Not certain she had understood her father correctly, Tatiana asked him to repeat it and he distinctly said: 'Sonya, on Sonya, so many things fall on her.' 'Do you want to see Sonya?', she asked, ready to break the taboo against admitting her.[7] He did not answer. There is also a recently publicized family legend that Tolstoy did once express the wish to see his wife, but there is no way to verify this.

We know that the decision not to tell Tolstoy about his wife's arrival was taken by the people surrounding him, who wanted to protect the old man from excessive and possibly fatal emotions. They may have been right, but they did not give him a choice. Likewise, he was not told about the arrival of a monk from Optina Pustyn' on a mission to try to convince him to reconcile with the Church. There is little doubt that Tolstoy's answer would have been negative, but once again he was deprived of the possibility to decide for himself.

Sofia peeping in the window to see the dying Tolstoy, November 1910.

Tolstoy was subjected to intensive medical treatment. He had never believed in medicine, considering it, at best, useless for the sick and especially for the dying, but he believed it was helpful for those around the sick and dying because it afforded them an illusion of meaningful activity. Sometimes he objected to specific medicines and procedures, asking the doctors 'not to jostle him' and 'not to bother him' (*Mak*, IV, p. 426), but in general he was an obedient and obliging patient. There was one thing, though, that he resisted vehemently: morphine injections.

Apart from his aversion to all kinds of intoxication, Tolstoy had a more intimate and existential reason to object to any sedation with opiates. Throughout his life he had been thinking about death, preparing himself for this solemn moment and had often expressed his desire to experience this most important transition while fully conscious. He was denied that chance.

Dying proved to be difficult for him. His body was struggling against the inevitable. On the eve of his death he agreed to an injection only when he was convinced that he was going to be treated with camphor, not morphine. He called his son Sergei and, with growing difficulty, said: 'Seriozha, Truth, love much, love all' (*Mak*, IV, p. 430). Different memoirists recall this sentence in different ways, but its meaning was clear to everyone. At 11 p.m., when everyone except for the doctors on duty had gone to bed, Tolstoy said: 'How hard it is to die, one should live a godly life.' Half an hour later, believing his persistent hiccups were a danger to his heart, Dr Makovitsky suggested he take morphine. 'I do not want parffin,' Tolstoy replied, confusing the words 'morphine' and 'parffin' [paraffin]. Towards midnight, however, a dose of the drug was injected. Makovitsky observes that a quarter of an hour later a half-delirious Tolstoy muttered: 'I am going somewhere, so that no one can bother (or find) [me], Leave me in peace . . . It is time to scarper. It is time to scarper' (*Mak*, IV, pp. 430–31). These were his last words.

The meticulous Makovitsky put the words 'or find' in brackets to indicate that he might have misheard one word in the phrase

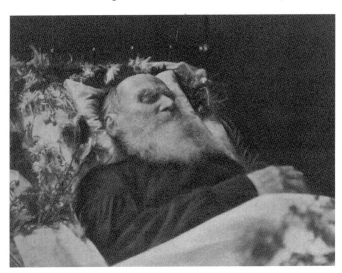

Tolstoy on his deathbed.

'no one can bother me'. The Russian words *nashol* ('find') and *meshal* ('bother') do sound similar, but the significance of these alternatives is more or less irrelevant. Just as he had done eighty years before, when two caring grown-ups stood over his bed and watched while his arms were bound in swaddling, Tolstoy was protesting against suffocating control. But there was one difference this time. Now he had the chance to 'scarper'. He used this chance the next morning, on 7 November, at 6.05 a.m.

References

1 An Ambitious Orphan

1 Philippe Lejeune, *On Diary*, ed. Jeremy D. Popkin and Julie Rak (Honolulu, HI, 2009), p. 179.
2 P. V. Annenkov, *Literaturnye Vospominania* (Moscow, 1983), p. 522.
3 S. A. Tolstaya, 'Tri biograficheskikh ocherka Tolstogo', *Literaturnoe nasledstvo*, LXIX (1961), p. 508.
4 L. N. Tolstoy, *Polnoe sobranie sochinenii v sta tomah* (Moscow, 2002), II, pp. 393–4.
5 A. A. Fet, *Moi vospominaniia, 1848–1889* (Moscow, 1890), vol. I, p. 106.
6 V. S. Morozov, 'Vospominaniia uchenika iasnopolianskoi shkoly', in *L. N. Tolstoy v vospominaniiakh sovremennikov* (Moscow, 1960), vol. I, p. 110.

2 A Married Genius

1 N. A. Nekrasov, *Polnoe sobranie sochinenii i pisem v piatnadtsati tomakh* (Leningrad, 1972), vol. IV, p. 83.
2 Leo Tolstoy, *War and Peace: Original Version*, trans. Andrew Bromfield (London, 2007), pp. 872–3.
3 Ilya Tolstoy, *Tolstoy: My Father: Reminiscences*, trans. Ann Dunnigan (London, 1972), p. 56.
4 Trans. Alex Wilbraham.
5 Ilya Tolstoy, *Tolstoy, My Father*, p. 60.
6 A. A. Fet, *Polnoe sobranie stikhotvorenii* (Leningrad, 1959), p. 360.
7 Arthur Schopenhauer, *The World as Will and Representation*, trans. E.F.J. Payne (New York, 1966), vol. II, pp. 573–4.
8 *Perepiska L. N. Tolstogo s N. N. Strakhovym, 1870–1894* (St Petersburg, 1914), p. 55.
9 Schopenhauer, *The World as Will and Representation*, vol. II, p. 557.

10 E. V. Obolenskaya, 'Moia mat' i Lev Nikolaevich', in *Letopisi gosudarstvennogo literaturnogo muzeia* (Moscow, 1938), vol. II, p. 279.

11 Schopenhauer, *The World as Will and Representation*, vol. II, p. 558.

12 Nekrasov, *Polnoe sobranie sochinenii*, vol. III, p. 72.

13 E. G. Babaev, *Lev Tolstoi i russkaia zhurnalistika ego epokhi* (Moscow, 1993), p. 133.

3 A Lonely Leader

1 Lidya Ginzburg, *Notes from the Blockade* (London, 2016), p. 21.

2 A. N. Wilson, *Tolstoy* (London, 2012), p. 325.

3 V. F. Bulgakov, *Poslednii god zhizni Tolstogo* (Moscow, 1960), p. 229.

4 S. A. Tolstoy letter to T. A. Kuzminskaya, 10 December 1874 (Archive of Tolstoy Museum in Moscow).

5 K. P. Pobedonostsev, *Pis'ma Pobedonostseva Aleksandru III* (Moscow, 1926), vol. II, p. 253.

6 Cited in John Simmons, *Leo Tolstoy* (London, 1949), p. 523.

7 L. D. Opul'skaya, *L. N. Tolstoy: Materialy k biografii s 1892 po 1899 god.* (Moscow, 1998), p. 139.

8 Ivan Bunin, *The Liberation of Tolstoy* (Evanston, IL, 2001), p. 50. Bunin mistakenly referred to Tolstoy's sick son as 'Kolia'.

9 A. B. Goldenveizer, *Vblizi Tolstogo* (Moscow, 1959), p. 57.

10 F. I. Tiutchev, *Polnoe sobranie stikhotovorenii* (Leningrad, 1987), p. 127 [trans. Alex Wilbraham].

11 P. P. Gnedich, 'Iz zapisnoi knizhki', in *Tolstoy v vospominaniakh sovremennikov* (Moscow, 1960), I, p. 534.

12 Opul'skaya, *L. N. Tolstoy: Materialy*, p. 112.

13 E. V. Obolenskaya, 'Moia mat' i Lev Nikolaevich', in *Letopisi gosudarstvennogo literaturnogo muzeia* (Moscow, 1938), vol. II, p. 299.

14 Ibid., p. 315.

15 A. M. Gorky, 'Lev Tolstoy', *Tolstoy v vospominaniakh sovremennikov*, vol. II, pp. 431, 450.

16 M. Gorky and R. Rolland, *Perepiska* (Moscow, 1996), pp. 87–8.

17 S. L. Tolstoy, *Ocherki bylogo* (Tula, 1965), p. 227.

18 Obolenskaya, 'Moia mat' i Lev Nikolaevich', p. 302.

19 Tatyana Tolstoy, *Tolstoy Remembered* (London, 1977), p. 164.

20 *Lev Nikolaevich Tolstoy. Yubileinyi sbornik* (Moscow–Leningrad, 1928), pp. 91–2.

21 Goldenveizer, *Vblizi Tolstogo*, p. 234.

4 A Fugitive Celebrity

1 E. I. Popov, 'Ortryvochnye vospominaniia o L've Tolstom', in *Letopisi gosudarstvennogo literaturnogo muzeia* (Moscow, 1938), vol. II, p. 367.

2 Tatyana Tolstoy, *Tolstoy Remembered* (London, 1977), p. 180.

3 A. A. Blok, *Sobranie sochinenii* (Moscow and Leningrad, 1963), vol. VII, p. 87.

4 E. E. Gorbunova-Posadova, *Drug Tolstogo–Maria Aleksandrovna Schmidt* (Moscow, 1929), p. 95.

5 E. V. Obolenskaya, 'Moia mat' i Lev Nikolaevich', in *Letopisi gosudarstvennogo literaturnogo muzeia* (Moscow, 1938), vol. II, p. 314.

6 V. B. Remizov, *Ukhod Tolstogo* (Moscow, 2017), p. 506.

7 Tatyana Tolstoy, *Tolstoy Remembered*, p. 241.

Select Bibliography

Tolstoy's Works

Anna Karenina, trans. George Gibian (London and New York, 1995)
Childhood, Boyhood, Youth, trans. Dora O'Brien (Richmond, 2006)
The Cossacks and Other Early Stories, trans. Louise and Aylmer Maude
    (Ware, 2012)
The Death of Ivan Ilyich and Other Stories, trans. Nicolas Pasternak Slater
    (Oxford, 2015)
Divine and Human and Other Stories, trans. Peter Sekirin (London, 2001)
The Gospel in Brief, trans. Isabel Hapgood (London, 2010)
Hadji Murat, trans. Kyril Zinovieff and Jenny Hughes (Richmond, 2015)
Leo Tolstoy: Spiritual Writings (New York, 2006)
Resurrection, trans. Aylmer Maude (Ware, 1999)
Polnoe sobranie sochinenii, 90 vols (Moscow, 1928–64)
Tolstoy's Diaries, trans. R. F. Christian (London, 1994)
Tolstoy's Letters, trans. R. F. Christian, 2 vols (New York, 1978)
Tolstoy's Political Thought (London, 2012)
Tolstoy's Short Fiction, trans. Michael Katz (London and New York, 2008)
Tolstoy as Teacher: Leo Tolstoy's Writings on Education, trans. Christopher
    Edgar (New York, 2000)
War and Peace, trans. George Gibian (London and New York, 1996)
War and Peace: Original Version, trans. Andrew Bromfield (London, 2007)

Biographical Materials

Bulgakov, Valentin, *Last Year of Lev Tolstoy*, ed. and trans. Ann Dunnigan
    (London, 1971)
Bunin, Ivan, *The Liberation of Tolstoy*, trans. Thomas Gaiton Marullo and
    Vladimir T. Khmelkov (Evanston, IL, 2001)

Chertkov, V. G., *The Last Days of Tolstoy*, trans. Nathalie A. Duddington (London, 1922)

Gol'denveĭzer, A. B., *Talks with Tolstoy*, trans. S. S. Koteliansky and Virginia Woolf (Richmond, 1923)

Gorky's Tolstoy and Other Reminiscences, trans. Donald Fanger (New Haven, CT, 2008)

Kuzminskaya, Tatiana, *Moia zhizn' doma i v Yasnoi Polyane* (Tula, 1973)

Makovitsky, Dushan, 'U Tolstogo, 1904–1910: Yasnopolianskie zapiski', *Literaturnoe nasledstvo*, XC/1–4 (1979)

Sukhotin-Tolstoy, Tatiana, *The Tolstoy Home*, trans. Alec Brown (London, 1950)

Tolstoy, Alexandra, *Tolstoy: A Life of My Father*, trans. Elizabeth Reynolds (London, 1953)

Tolstoy, Ilya, *Tolstoy: My Father: Reminiscences*, trans. Ann Dunnigan (London, 1972)

Tolstoy, Sofia, *The Diaries*, trans. Cathy Porter (Richmond, 1977)

Tolstaya, Sofia Andreevna, *Literary Works* (Moscow, 2011)

Tolstoy, Tatiana, *Tolstoy Remembered* (London, 1977)

Inteview i besedy s L'vom Tolstym (Moscow, 1986)

Perepiska Tolstogo s russkimi pisateliami, ed. S. Rozanova, 2 vols (Moscow, 1978)

Perepiska L. N. Tolstogo s N. N. Strakhovym, 1870–1894 (St Petersburg, 1914)

L. N. Tolstoy i A. A. Tolstaya: Perepiska, 1857–1903 (Moscow, 2011)

Tolstaya, Sofia, *Pis'ma L. N. Tolstomu* (Moscow and Leningrad, 1936)

——, *Dnevniki*, 2 vols (Moscow, 1978)

——, *Moia zhizn'*, 2 vols (Moscow, 2011)

Biographical Works

Bartlett, Rosamund, *Tolstoy: A Russian Life* (London, 2010)

Basinskii, Pavel, *Lev Tolstoi: begstvo iz raia* (Moscow, 2011)

Briggs, Anthony, *Leo Tolstoy* (London, 2010)

Maude, Aulmer, *The Life of Tolstoy* (Ware, 2008)

Nikitina, Nina, *Povsednevnaya zhizn' L'va Tolstogo v Yasnoi Polyane* (Moscow, 2007)

Popoff, Alexandra, *Tolstoy's False Disciple: The Untold Story of Leo Tolstoy and Vladimir Chertkov* (New York, 2014)

Remizov, V. B., *Ukhod Tolstogo, kak eto bylo* (Moscow, 2017)

Shklovskii, Victor, *Lev Tolstoy*, trans. Olga Shartse (Moscow, 1988)

Simmons, Ernest J., *Leo Tolstoy* (London, 1949)

Wilson, A. N., *Tolstoy* (London, 2012)

Zverev, Aleksei, and Vladimir Tunimanov, *Lev Tolstoy* (Moscow, 2006)

Secondary Literature

Aleksandrov, Vladimir E., *Limits to Interpretation: The Meanings of Anna Karenina* (Madison, WI, 2004)

Babaev, E. G., *Lev Tolstoĭ i russkaiā zhurnalistika ego epokhi* (Moscow, 1978

Bayley, John, *Tolstoy and the Novel* (London, 1968)

Berlin, Isaiah, *The Hedgehog and the Fox: An Essay on Tolstoy's View of History* (London, 2014)

Berman, Anna A., *Siblings in Tolstoy and Dostoevsky: The Path to Universal Brotherhood* (Evanston, IL, 2015)

Blakesley, Rosalind P., *Russia and the Arts: The Age of Tolstoy and Tchaikovsky* (London, 2016)

Bocharov, S. G., *Roman L. Tolstogo 'Voĭna i mir'* (Moscow, 1963)

Christian, R. F., *Tolstoy's 'War and Peace': A Study* (Oxford, 1962)

——, *Tolstoy: A Critical Introduction* (Cambridge, 1969)

Eikhenbaum, Boris, *Tolstoi in the Sixties*, trans. Duffield White (Ann Arbor, MI, 1982)

Eikhenbaum, B. M., *Raboty o L've Tolstom* (St Petersburg, 2009)

Feuer, Kathryn B., *Tolstoy and the Genesis of 'War and Peace'* (Ithaca, NY, and London, 1996)

Fodor, Alexander, *Tolstoy and the Russians: Reflections on a Relationship* (Ann Arbor, MI, 1984)

——, *The Quest for a Non-violent Russia: The Partnership of Leo Tolstoy and Vladimir Chertkov* (Lanham, MD, and London, 1989)

Fusso, Susan, *Editing Turgenev, Dostoevsky, and Tolstoy: Mikhail Katkov and the Great Russian Novel* (DeKalb, IL, 2017)

Ginzburg, Lydia, *On Psychological Prose*, trans. Judson Rosengrant (Princeton, NJ, 1991)

Gustafson, Richard. F., *Leo Tolstoy, Resident and Stranger: A Study in Fiction and Theology* (Princeton, NJ, 2014)

Knapp, Liza, *Anna Karenina and Others: Tolstoy's Labyrinth of Plots*
    (Madison, WI, 2016)
Knowles, A. V., ed., *Leo Tolstoy: The Critical Heritage*
    (London, 1997)
LeBlanc, Ronald. D., *Vegetarianism in Russia: The Tolstoy(an) Legacy*
    (Pittsburgh, PA, 2001)
Lukács, George, *Studies in European Realism: A Sociological Survey of the
    Writings of Balzac, Stendhal, Zola, Tolstoy, Gorki, and Others*
    (New York, 1964)
McLean, Hugh, *In Quest of Tolstoy* (Boston, MA, 2008)
McPeak, Rick, and Donna Tussing Orwin, *Tolstoy on War: Narrative Art
    and Historical Truth in 'War and Peace'* (Ithaca, NY, and London, 2012)
Maiorova, Olga, *From the Shadow of Empire: Defining the Russian Nation
    through Cultural Mythology, 1855–1870* (Madison, WI, 2010)
Mandelker, Amy, *Framing Anna Karenina: Tolstoy, the Woman Question,
    and the Victorian Novel* (Columbus, OH, 1993)
Medzhibovskaya, Inessa, *Tolstoy and the Religious Culture of His Time:
    A Biography of a Long Conversion, 1845–1887* (Lanham, MD, 2009)
——, ed., *Tolstoy and His Problems: Views from the Twenty-first Century*
    (De Kalb, IL, 2018)
Møller, Peter Ulf, *Postlude to the Kreutzer Sonata: Tolstoy and the Debate on
    Sexual Morality in Russian Literature in the 1890s* (Leiden and New York,
    1988)
Morson, Gary Saul, *Hidden in Plain View: Narrative and Creative Potentials in
    'War and Peace'* (Stanford, CA, 1987)
Nickell, William, *The Death of Tolstoy: Russia on the Eve, Astapovo Station,
    1910* (Ithaca, NY, 2010)
Orekhanov, Georgii, *Lev Tolstoi 'Prorok bez chesti': Khronika. Katastrofy*
    (Moscow, 2016)
Orwin, Donna Tussing, *Tolstoy's Art and Thought, 1847–1880* (Princeton,
    NJ, 1993)
——, ed., *The Cambridge Companion to Tolstoy* (Cambridge, 2002)
——, ed., *Anniversary Essays on Tolstoy* (Cambridge and New York, 2010)
Paperno, Irina, *'Who, what am I?': Tolstoy Struggles to Narrate the Self*
    (Ithaca, NY, and London, 2014)
Peace, Richard, *Tolstoy's Three Great Novels: An Analysis* (Bristol, 2010)

Rancour-Laferriere, Daniel, *Tolstoy on the Couch: Misogyny, Masochism and the Absent Mother* (Basingstoke, 1998)

Shklovsky, Viktor, *Mater'ial i stil' v romane L'va Tolstogo 'Voĭna i Mir'* (The Hague, 1970)

Steiner, George, *Tolstoy or Dostoevsky* (Harmondsworth, 1967)

Wasiolek, Edward, *Critical Essays on Tolstoy* (Boston, MA, 1986)

——, *Tolstoy's Major Fiction* (Chicago, IL, and London, 1978)

Acknowledgements

I want to express my deepest gratitude to Alex Wilbraham and Arkady Ostrovsky for their generous support and help in the long process of writing this short book. Mikhail Dolbilov kindly read the manuscript and provided valuable remarks and suggestions. The colleagues at Tolstoy Museum in Moscow and Yasnaya Polyana were incredibly generous and supportive of my work. As always, I am grateful to my wife Irina Zorina for her help and encouragement.

When I was young, I used to discuss Tolstoy with my closest friend Boris (Barukh) Berman (1957–1992), who was then an aspiring Tolstoy scholar. He tragically died in a car accident near Jerusalem. His several remaining articles on Tolstoy were published posthumously. I do not think he would have agreed with everything I say and cannot even be sure he would have liked this book at all. Still his intellectual passion and personal integrity served as a major source of inspiration for me. Remembering our unforgettable conversations, I want to dedicate my book to his memory.

Photo Acknowledgements

The author and publishers wish to express their thanks to the below sources of illustrative material and/or permission to reproduce it. While every effort has been made to identify and credit copyright holders, we would like to apologize to anyone who has not been formally acknowledged.

L. N. Tolstoy State Museum, Moscow: pp. 9 (photo M. Panov), 12, 19, 20, 21 (photo Sofia Tolstoy), 37 (photo S. Levitsky), 55, 56 (photo P. Sergeenko), 62, 63, 77, 84, 95 (photo F. Khodasevich), 117 (photo P. Preobrazhensky), 127 (photo Y. Shteinberg), 128, 139 (photo E. Tomashevich), 146 (photo Sofia Tolstoy), 163 (photo Sofia Tolstoy), 165 (photo Sofia Tolstoy), 178 (photo M. Kurbatov), 181 (photo V. Chertkov), 190 (photo F. Protasevich), 192 (photo V. Chertkov), 198 (photo Sofia Tolstoy), 208, 209 (photo V. Chekhovsky) – these images are reproduced with the permission of the L. N. Tolstoy State Museum, Moscow, owners of the photographs; The Literary Museum of the Institute of Russian Literature, St Petersburg: p. 189; The Museum of the L. N. Tolstoy Estate, Yasnaya Polyana: pp. 34 (photo A. Shurlepov), 143 (photo I. Guschin), 206 (photo I. Guschin); photo enlarged and retouched from a frame of Pate Brothers company newsreel film strip in the possession of the L.N. Tolstoy State Museum, Moscow, reproduced with their permission: p. 208; from an 1854 issue of *Russkii Khudozhestvennyi Listok*: p. 31; State Tretyakov Gallery, Moscow: p. 121.